Showers of Blessing

by
Pearl Steinkuehler
and
Matilda Nordtvedt

moody press
CHICAGO

©1980 by
THE MOODY BIBLE INSTITUTE
OF CHICAGO

Library of Congress Cataloging in Publication Data

Nordtvedt, Matilda.
    Showers of blessing.

    1. Showers (Parties)   2. Infants' supplies.
I. Steinkuehler, Pearl, joint author.   II. Title.
GV1472.7.S5N67   793.2   80-19764
ISBN 0-8024-0434-0

        5 6 7 Printing/LC/Year 90 89 88 87 86

        Printed in the United States of America

CONTENTS

1

Baby Showers—A Ministry

"Oh, no, not another baby shower!" you wail. "That's the fifth one in three months!"

You can take that attitude and grudgingly buy another baby gift because you *have to*, or you can look upon baby showers as a special kind of ministry. That cup of cold water given to one of His little ones that Jesus talked about in Matthew 10:42 is symbolic of other necessities as well: diapers, shirts, safety pins, and sleepers that we give at a shower to help a new mother clothe and care for her baby.

Who? Some churches have rules as to who merits a baby shower. Are the parents members? Are they staying around after the baby comes, or will they be moving away? Those who are not members or who are moving away (such as students) sometimes do not rate a shower. After all, what return can they make to the church?

That attitude contradicts the teachings of Jesus. Didn't He tell His disciples to be hospitable to those who could not return the favor (Luke 14:13-14)? Wouldn't that apply to showers as well?

Lori was a newcomer to the church and did not know many of the people. She was expecting a baby. What better way would there be to get to know Lori and make her feel welcome in the church family than to have a baby shower for her?

Jeanette and her husband were university students, planning to move on after graduation. Who needs a shower for their baby more than a couple of students?

Giving a shower in love is one way to show the love of Christ to newcomers and transients. A young girl was honored by a shower. She soon left the city, was eventually caught in the web of divorce and misery, and dropped out of church for a while. What brought Dortha back to the Lord and to a new, worthwhile life for herself and her young son? The memory of a church that cared enough for a young transient to give her a baby shower!

Teresa, a young mother from Korea, was happy for friendship from some American Christians. When expecting her second baby, her friends surprised her with a baby shower, something she had never heard of in her country but that delighted her immensely. The shower, expressing Christian love, was one small link in the chain that eventually brought Teresa to a personal relationship with Jesus Christ.

When? Ask the expectant mother if she would prefer the shower before or after the child is born. Alice had miscarried so many times she was not sure she could have a healthy baby. She asked us to have the shower after the baby was born.

Jan preferred that too, but for a different reason. She wanted her friends to know whether to buy blue or pink. If her shower had come before the baby was born, her little Kari wouldn't have all those darling frilly dresses now.

Some new mothers, however, feel overwhelmed by all there is to buy for the new baby: diapers, pins, sleepers, shirts, bibs, blankets. They prefer the shower before the baby is born. In such cases it is wise for some of the guests to choose larger sizes of those items. What would a mother do with sixteen newborn-to-three-month sleepers?

What? A "needle shower," a "baby bath shower," or a "lady-in-waiting" shower can be given. Some simple games, a short devotional, and then the gifts and refreshments are all that are needed.

Showers can be a time of fellowship and fun. They can meet an important need. They should be a ministry done as unto the Lord. This book is designed to help you decide what kind of shower you would like to give, and to make the giving of "another shower" a joy to all concerned

2

Make Your Shower *Different!*

What kind of shower will you have? Many things will determine your choice. You can do the same old thing you've always done, or you can mix and match these ideas with some you already have to produce something new and refreshing. Enjoy the variety!

Dos and Don'ts

Anything worth doing is worth doing right. Please do not plan to be a one-woman show at any of your showers. Involve others in the planning and performing of the task.

Having several committees will make it easier for all involved: program, publicity, decorating, food, and cleanup. The program committee plans the games, program, and gift presentation. The publicity committee is responsible for inviting guests. The decorating committee sees that the shower decor is done and is in keeping with the program committee's plans. The food committee decides what to serve. Refreshments also should be coordinated with the program plans. The clean-up committee washes the dishes and returns the meeting room to its former state.

If you have a small group, a committee can easily be one person. Pity poor Paula if she gets stuck with the total package!

Remember: to fail to plan is to plan to fail. The following are suggestions to help you make your baby showers a success.

NEEDLE SHOWER

This shower is unique in that each person attending brings her needle. Of course that's not all; she brings scissors, thimble, thread, cloth, and patterns, too. Perhaps two or more women will bring portable sewing machines.

At a needle shower the guests pitch in and sew a layette for the baby. A variation could be to embroider blocks for a baby quilt that the hostess will finish later.

Just before the refreshments, a short devotion can be given using ideas in the section on program helps. Relate the following anecdote to the ladies. Needles have been of utmost importance in cold countries because of the necessity of people's making clothing for themselves and their families. The Eskimos and other people of Arctic regions valued their needles so highly they kept them in jeweled cases when not in use. In Yukaghir, Siberia, an appropriate gift for a baby girl was needles. They were kept for her in a little bag until she was old enough to use them.

A "MA BELL" SHOWER

Has a special mother-to-be moved away before you could honor her with a shower? Have a shower anyway with the honoree in absentia.

Gather guests, unwrapped gifts, and goodies and call the honoree to tell her the party is in her honor. Let each talk with her for a few moments. After good-byes, gift wrap and package up the presents. Then write her a long letter full of details about her party.

The conversation with far away friends will probably be the best appreciated gift of all!

FOR A MISSIONARY BABY

Is one of your missionary friends having a baby? How about

giving her a long-distance shower? Friends gather at someone's home with unwrapped gifts for the baby, which are passed around so all can see. Then the women wrap the gifts and prepare them for mailing.

A letter from the missionary could be read and special prayer offered for the new mother and coming baby. Make a tape on which each guest gives the missionary mother a greeting, a Bible verse, and a piece of advice on mothering.

POST OFFICE SHOWER

Does your recreation area have a serving window? Convert it into a Babyland Post Office window. Outline the window with twisted pink and blue crepe paper streamers. Arrange large letters made from pink and blue construction paper (or baby gift-wrap paper) that read "Babyland Post Office" over the window. Scales for weighing gifts and letters may stand on the counter. One of the hostesses will act as "postmistress" and encourage guests to "mail" their gifts at the window. Before the party, ask guests to prepare letters of advice for the new mom. Encourage them also to make predictions of the date, hour, and minute of the expected new arrival. Post the "letters" as they arrive, also.

Carry out the post office idea in games and refreshments. For instance, the one who predicts the arrival facts the most accurately can be "volunteered" for the first babysitter the new mom will need. A cake decorated as a special delivery package would be appropriate.

The postmistress will distribute the gifts and letters, of course. A fitting extra gift from the hostesses could be a book of stamps the new mom will need to mail announcements about the new arrival!

A DOUBLE FEATURE SHOWER

Are two ladies you care about expecting babies about the same time? Plan a double shower, but keep it a surprise to the honorees.

10

Invite each mother-to-be to a surprise shower for the other, but clue all the guests into the double feature plan.

"It's Twins!"

Has your honoree been told by her doctor that hers is to be a multiple birth? Or have her twins already arrived? Then host an "It's Twins!" shower.

Have two that match of everything. Guests can shop together or each can get two of whatever she gives. Decorate the party room with pictures of twins, clipped from magazines.

Play games dealing with twins. See chapter 5 for name games and "Double Talk." Try a relay in which each team tries to diaper a doll in record time.

Double up on refreshments, too. A cake with twin babies on top would be cute.

A Living Doll

In this shower, care is taken to center the gift items on completely dressing an expected baby. To avoid duplicates, guests are asked in advance to contribute a certain amount of money toward the gifts. Funds are pooled, and several ladies go shopping together to complete an outfit for the baby. The hostesses dress a large doll in the outfit and put her in a bassinet as a party decoration.

After games have been played, it is revealed to the honoree that she has been gazing at her gifts all evening. The doll is then passed and each guest removes one article of clothing. A corner table is then uncovered to reveal boxes, paper, and ribbons. Ladies are to select what they need to wrap the clothing item they hold. The mother-to-be acts as judge to select the most artistically wrapped gift and the gift best disguising the contents of the package. The honoree will take home the wrapped gifts so her husband can enjoy with her the outfits to clothe their "living doll." (If the baby has not yet been born, make arrangements with the department store to exchange items of clothing that may have been selected for the wrong sex.)

As a final gift, make arrangements with a local photographer for a gift certificate to take a portrait of the "living doll."

MOTHER-CHILD SHOWER

Bring your preschoolers with you to the party and avoid the baby-sitting problem. Children love babies and will add zest to the gathering. Include the children in prizes, games, and food (simple finger food). Let children distribute the gifts to the honoree. If any of them have babies at their houses, they may be asked to tell the honoree what they like best about their babies and how they help Mommy take care of their babies.

SIMULTANEOUS SHOWERS

While the women honor the mother-to-be, have a shower for the dad-to-be at the same time but at a different place. While the women do the traditional shower things, an outgoing dad can lead the men to be of real help to the one they're welcoming into the realm of fatherhood.

Invite the men to give the new father things he'll need to diaper the baby. Experienced dads can give advice on how to handle emergencies like two A.M. feedings and colic. Add a sporty feature as fathers compete with a stopwatch to see which relay team can diaper a doll in record time.

Dads should serve man-size food to fortify them for the task of fathering. "Hero" sandwiches and strong coffee should suffice.

A COUPLE'S SHOWER

Invite couples to enjoy this special time together. Emphasize the fact that husband and wife are in this family project together. Have couples work together on some games. Plan several "guys versus gals" competitions, too. Two guys who are good sports might compete with a baby bottle race while the others cheer them on (see chapter 5).

At gift-opening time, the father-to-be will guess what is in the package before his wife opens it.

POST PARTUM
BLUES-AWAY SHOWER

Bring your good wishes to the hospital. Based on the theory that "a gift a day will keep the blues away," gather just a few friends to bring some gifts for mother and baby to be opened in the hospital—one each day.

Gifts may not be a medically prescribed way to prevent the post partum doldrums, but a daily reminder of "we love you" is bound to be uplifting to the spirit.

BABY ANIMALS

Decorate your shower setting with pictures of baby animals and stuffed animal toys. Grace the gift table with a big teddy bear. Serve a cake shaped like an animal (see chapter 7). Make punch festive by floating ice molds made in animal-shaped cookie cutters.

Include among your games "Animal Babies" (chapter 5). Give the game winner a miniature stuffed animal to be given to the new baby.

Conclude this theme with meditations from several of the "Animal Babies" devotionals in the program helps.

MEMORIES

Focus on memorable days from the guests' childhood. Decorate with pictures and items that were dear to the guests' past. If any have dolls, clothes, or toys from their babyhood or the childhood of their own children, encourage them to bring them and share their significance with those at the shower. Share also memories of showers that guests may have had.

Help the new mother begin making memories by preparing for her a scrapbook of her shower (chapter 8). A talented lady can make her an original gift of a memory shadow box. Suggestions for that are in Chapter 8 also. Surprise the mother with an extra gift—a jar of baby food from each guest. Ask them to label the jars with the donor's name for a pleasant memory of the shower when the food is used by the baby months later.

Play "Whose Child is This?" "Bible Names" would be an appropriate memory game also (see chapter 5).

Does a guest have an antique buggy, cradle, or bassinet? If so, fill it with the gifts for the honoree.

Cover the serving table with an old lace cloth and serve refreshments on old china or crystal dishes.

The Building Blocks Cake served on a cake plate on a stand would be lovely. Make tiny baby buggies from candy orange slices for take-home favors (see chapter 7).

Play "Memories" and other old records as background music during refreshments.

Entertain with the poem "What Might Have Been" (chapter 4).

A fitting conclusion to this theme would be "Dare We Bring a Baby into Today's World?" (chapter 3).

ON THE WING

For a springtime shower, build your theme around the winged creatures. Collect figurines, pictures, and paintings of colorful birds and butterflies for decorating the room where the shower will be held. Encourage those invited to the shower to bring their canaries and parakeets along for "atmosphere."

Hang a pretty musical bird mobile over the gift table. Give the mobile to the mother for her new baby's crib.

You may want to use the stork as decorations on refreshments. Make reference to eagles, hummingbirds, and killdeer in the "Animal Babies" devotional (see chapter 4). Conclude with thoughts about the wisdom of the swallow's rearing her young in the church, God's eye being on the sparrow, and His declaration that our worth is far above that of the insignificant sparrow He protects (Matthew 10:29-31). Plan for a soloist to sing a medley of "He's Got the Whole World in His Hands" and "His Eye Is on the Sparrow."

THE PRINTED WORD

Center this shower on books and their influence on mothers and babies. Ask each guest to bring a book they have found helpful in their homes. Ask them to tell why the book helped them. Decorate the room with book jackets borrowed from your local or church library.

Does one of your ladies have a book-shaped cake pan? She could prepare your cake and decorate the book like a baby book.

On the gift table, arrange some of the book-shaped packages between bookends. Use Praying Hands bookends if possible. Prepare a low centerpiece book for the gift table from directions found in chapter 9. Give this styrofoam or découpaged book to the honoree for a keepsake.

Conclude with a devotional on the Holy Book as the best help for child-rearing. (see "The Final Word" in chapter 3, "Program Helps"). Give the mother a small New Testament for her baby and *The Christian Family* by Larry Christenson.*

---

*Minneapolis: Bethany Fellowship, 1978.

SHOWERS OF FLOWERS

Major on flowers for this shower. Invitations can be on prepared cards decorated with gummed forget-me-nots. Make the room fragrant and lovely with fresh flowers everywhere. Intersperse arrangements in borrowed bootee and cradle vases with arrangements in borrowed baby shoes. To keep the flowers in the shoes fresh, insert a small glass of water in each shoe to hold the flowers. Use further decorating ideas from "Flower Shower" in chapter 6.

Give the honoree a corsage of fresh or artificial flowers; add a chenille-stemmed "baby" or a small rattle.

Play "Bouquet for Baby" (chapter 6).

BATHE THE BABY

This type of shower is best suited to a small group of ladies. By previous arrangement with the new mother, guests gather in the morning to watch the baby have his/her bath. A new mother might appreciate having an experienced mother offer her tips on how to bathe the baby without "breaking" it.

After the baby is bathed and fed, the ladies can prepare a brunch from food items they have brought. When the brunch is finished, present the new mother with gifts for the baby.

LADY-IN-WAITING SHOWER

This is a different kind of shower in that the expectant mother rather than the expected baby, receives the gifts. This is especially appropriate for a second, third, or fourth child. Guests bring gifts for the expectant mother to use during those last difficult days of waiting, while she is in the hospital, and when she first gets home.

Inexpensive gifts such as stationery, bath powder, cologne, undies, or a good book would be appropriate. Or guests could pool their money to buy a new nightie, robe, and slippers for the mother-to-be.

BABY POTLUCK

Having a potluck lunch for which each guest (except the honoree) brings one dish to share. Give the new mother gifts of money in cards, regular baby gifts, or go together and buy a large gift such as a high chair or stroller.

GRANDMOTHER SHOWER

Is one of your friends expecting a first grandchild? You may want to honor her with a grandmother shower. She'll be delighted to open the gifts and pass them on to her new grandchild. This is especially appropriate if the expectant mother lives far away or you do not know her well enough to give her a shower.

Use the "Great Grandmother" devotional in chapter 3. Read "What's in a Name?" and "How Do You Tell a Gramma When You See One?" from the poetry chapter. Play the Grandmother game in chapter 5.

Besides gifts for the baby, give the honoree a Grandma Brag Book.

LULLABY AND GOODNIGHT

Feature the lullaby in this unique shower. The dictionary defines lullaby as "a song to quiet children or lull them to sleep."

When inviting ladies to this shower, ask each to recall a lullaby they sang or had sung to them as babies. Plan to share those at the shower. It will be especially interesting if women come from different parts of the United States or from several countries of the world. Plan to set the atmosphere of this gathering by playing the most famous lullaby of all—Johannes Brahms's lullaby, "Wiegenlied," better known to us as "Lullaby and Goodnight."

"Music hath charms to soothe the savage beast," someone has said. Mothers have long used music to calm their crying babies.

Singing the lullaby is one of the sweetest parts of motherhood. A mother does not need a trained musical voice to delight her child and lull a baby to sleep with soft, loving sounds.

Crooning one's baby to sleep lends itself to musical creativity. The melody and words are not important if love sings. Some mothers present at the shower may entertain the others by singing to them some made-up lullabies they sang to their little ones. One mother confessed to singing a nondescript tune accompanied by the repetitive phrase "Go to sleep-y, little buttermilk baby." That strange lullaby worked wonders with her little girl, who fought sleep lest she miss some exciting family event.

A dozen or so lullabies from several cultures are included in the children's music book *Singing Together* (by Lilla Pitts, Mabelle Glenn, and Lorrain Watters; Boston: Ginn and Company, 1951). See if you can borrow some copies from your school library so your best singer can teach the mother-to-be (and the others, too) some of these lovely melodies.

An appropriate cake to accompany this theme could be a simple sheet cake adorned with a plastic bar of music and a sleeping baby in a bassinet (both decorations are available from a hobby or cake decorating store).

A fitting hostess gift to the honoree would be a music box or a musical crib mobile.

3

Program Helps

"Queen for a Day"
Program

In these days of nostalgia, it might be fun to pattern a shower program after the early television show "Queen for a Day." Pick several women to be contestants, the shower honoree among them. The contestants will have "tearjerker" stories about why they want to be queen, but the honoree will simply state that she is soon to have a baby and needs things for the wee one. By applause, guests will select the honoree to win.

The master of ceremonies may be a pretend Mrs. Jack Bailey who speaks through a real microphone or a pretend one (a potato stuck on a stick will do). The "queen" will be crowned with a pinned diaper having the leg holes pulled to stand up like peaks of a crown. Her robe will be a colorful receiving blanket, and her bouquet will be diapers rolled on cones like long-stemmed roses. Fete the "queen" with the gifts the guests have brought.

This program is a good one for a big group in which game playing would be cumbersome.

Conclude this fun program with a devotional thought or poem to lead the "queen" into a closer walk with King Jesus as He grants her the privilege of motherhood.

DID YOU KNOW?

We take our customs for granted, not often stopping to consider their origin. Here is a program for a baby shower that traces old beliefs and customs concerning babies.

BLUE FOR BOYS, PINK FOR GIRLS

Did you know that our custom of dressing boys in blue had its origin in fear of evil spirits? Ancient people believed demons were after their boy babies so they dressed them in the most potent color they knew—blue, the color of the heavens. They believed evil spirits were allergic to that color, so their baby boys would be safe if they were wearing it.

Baby girls were considered so inferior to boys that even the demons would not want them. Any old color would do for girls. Later, somebody thought baby girls should have a special color too and chose pink. [*]

BABY BUGGIES

Did you know that the baby buggy was not accepted in America when it was first invented? In 1848 Charles Burton made the first baby buggy and called it a perambulator ("pram" for short). People in New York condemned it as a traffic hazard. Mr. Burton took his invention to Britain. When Queen Victoria ordered the new baby carriage for her family, it caught on quickly. Queen Isabella of Spain and the Pasha of Egypt popularized it in their countries. Finally the United States was also convinced.

Today the smaller stroller has replaced the baby buggy to a great extent. [†]

SUPERSTITIONS ABOUT BABIES

Long ago parents believed that if they hid their child's cut hair, he

---

[*] R. Brasch, *How Did It Begin?* (New York: McKay, 1966), pp. 22-23.
[†] Ibid., pp. 23-24.

would be kept from bad luck. Some people hid it in church walls; others kept it under the thresholds of their houses. People of Thailand set it floating down the river in banana-leaf boats. Today we keep a lock of our baby's hair in a baby book, and it doesn't mean a thing except that we want to remember how soft it was.‡

Storks have been connected with the birth of babies since ancient times. People admired and loved storks because of their gentle ways with their mates and young. The German peasants encouraged storks to build nests on their roofs, thinking they would bring good luck. Storks love water and spend much of their time in marshes and ponds. Ancient people believed the souls of children lived in those wet places. It was easy to link the stork with childbearing.§

Some Indian tribes of Mexico are afraid to admit out loud that their baby is pretty or smart. Hoping to fool the evil spirits, they call their baby ugly and stupid. It is hoped the babies find out sooner or later what their mothers *really* think of them.

Did you know that:

Your baby will get straight A's if he is bald and has big feet?

He will be a good singer if he has a big mouth?

He will be generous if he has big ears?

He will be lucky if he has curly hair?

He will be *very* lucky if he is born with a full set of teeth?

He will rise in the world if you carry him up a flight of stairs before you carry him down?

A bag of chopped onions hung around his neck will ward off evil?

If you cut his fingernails before he is a year old he will become a thief? (Biting them is OK.)

Parents believed they could discover their child's future by putting the following objects on the floor before him: a spoon, a dollar, a book, a Bible, a baseball, a coin, and a diaper. If the baby picks up

‡Arthur S. Gregor, *Amulets, Talismans, and Fetishes* (New York: Scribner's, 1975), p. 12.

§R. Brasch, pp. 21-22.

the spoon he will be poor. If he chooses the dollar he will be rich. If he reaches for the book he will become a teacher, and if the Bible, he will become a preacher. If he goes for the baseball he will surely become an athlete, the coin a businessman, and the diaper a parent.‖

Although some of those superstitions are merely old wives' tales passed on from one generation to another, many of them have their origin in the fear of evil spirits.

When people became better educated they discounted evil spirits altogether. As Christians we know that evil spirits are real—fallen angels who followed Lucifer in rebellion against God. We have the assurance, however, that our God is stronger than Satan and his forces. God tells us in His Word that we need not fear "for greater is He who is in you than he who is in the world" (1 John 4:4).

Aren't you glad we can bring our children up in His love? John says, "There is no fear in love; but perfect love casts out fear" (1 John 4:18). Jesus said, "Let the children alone, and do not hinder them from coming to Me; for the kingdom of heaven belongs to such as these" (Matthew 19:14).

Let us praise Him now and ask His blessing on this little one who is coming or has come into our community. (*Lead in prayer.*)

"POT OF GOLD" QUIZ
PROGRAM

(*Master of ceremony "hams it up" with great dramatic pronouncements*)

MC: Good evening, ladies and gentlemen. This is Station BABY bringing you a program of quizzical fun, brought to you through the courtesy of "The Baby Layette Company." Win our pot of

‖Other baby customs from Alvin Schwartz, *Cross Your Fingers, Spit In Your Hat* (Philadelphia: Lippincott, 1974).

gold and then be eligible to win the "shower of prizes!" You can win this quiz by correctly answering the simple questions I will ask you.

We are now ready for our first contestant. What is your name, madam?

FIRST CONTESTANT: (*Gives name.*)

MC: So you want to try for our pot of gold! All right—your first question is: What is the difference between a rain cloud and a whipped child?

FIRST CONTESTANT: (*Answers.*)

MC: I'm sorry, but you did not give the right answer. The answer is: One pours with rain, while the other roars with pain.

Before we have our next contestant, let's go into the audience with baby pictures of some well-known celebrities and give you a chance at some of the prizes. (*Play game: "Whose Child Is This?" chapter 5*). (*Have a suitable poem read from chapter 4*).

MC: Now we are ready for our next contestant, _____ (*name*). Your question, my dear, for the pot of gold is: Why is a newborn baby like a gale of wind?

SECOND CONTESTANT: (*Answers.*)

MC: I'm sorry, but your answer is wrong also. The answer is: Because both begin with a squall.

Now, before we go on with the quiz, here are the Lullabiers to sing! (*Special music: "He's Got the Whole World in His Hands."*)

MC: Our next contestants are Mr. and Mrs. _____ (*honoree and husband*). Your question, Mr. _____, is: Who was the first baby?

FATHER-TO-BE: The first child ever born was Cain, the son of Adam and Eve.

MC: That is correct! You have won the pot of gold!! (*Presents the pot of gold, a little pink potty filled with new pennies.*) You are now ready to try for the "shower of prizes!" Here is your next question. Mrs. _____, you are to give us this answer. Talk it over with your husband, as we can accept only one answer. The question is: What people in this country still ride in buggies?

MOTHER-TO-BE: Babies.

23

MC: You are right! You have won the shower of prizes!! Congratulations to you!!! (*She presents the shower gifts to the parents-to-be.*)

(*After the gifts and refreshments are enjoyed, close with the following thoughts:*)

Gold has always been important to mankind. In fact, it is a necessity to buy that which we need to live. Wealth was a proof of God's blessing to the Hebrew people. But they considered children an even greater reward than wealth. Psalm 127:3 reads "Lo, children are an heritage of the LORD: and the fruit of the womb is his reward."

We rejoice with you in your inheritance from God, _____ and _____ (*honorees*). We are happy that soon you will be rewarded by the birth of one who will be more precious to you than gold. We are glad to share with you the gifts our gold has bought for you. We add this prayer that God will guide you as you lead this life more precious than gold. We pray that you and yours will one day walk the streets of gold, rejoicing with King Jesus.

WHAT'S IN A NAME?

Names are important. They distinguish one person from another, giving him or her an identity. Sometimes names have meanings, such as the names of our Lord as given to us in the Bible. Jesus, His best-known name, means *Savior*. Christ means the *Anointed One*, or *Messiah*.

In Bible times people gave their children names with significant meanings. Jacob's name means *cheat* or *supplanter*, because he grabbed his twin brother's heel as he was being born. Abraham means *father of many nations*, and Sarah means *princess*. Peter means a *rock*, and David, *beloved*.

Parents often give their children names of great people to inspire them to live nobly. Names of Bible greats have been popular for years: Daniel, John, Paul, James, Esther, Rachel, Deborah. Few people, if any, would name their child Judas, after the traitor of Jesus.

A child burdened with an odd or bizarre name may suffer emotional damage, because he will inevitably be teased by other children. Consider such combinations as Izah Crank, Faster Weedin, or Ineeda Coin. Hard-to-pronounce names can also become a burden to a child. Cute, lighthearted names are fun, but rob a child of dignity later in life. Candy or Cookie are cute names for a little girl, but a bit strange for a grandmother. Skip fits a freckle-faced little boy, but not the congressman he may become.

It is well for parents to consider the possible nickname of the name they choose for their child. One little girl I know liked her name, Delight, until the children at her school began calling her "Chicken Delight" after an advertised special at the drive-in.

Sometimes the combination of initials can be embarrassing, too. Bradford Allen Davis is a fine name, but who wants the initials B-A-D? Sally Ann Parsons sounds fine until you remember the initials spell S-A-P!

Jewish people often name their children after a loved one who has passed on. They feel that not only honors the deceased but gives their child roots in the past. Catholics give their children the name of a patron saint. Protestants often choose Bible names for their offspring. In Japan, Christians make up significant names for their children to express their faith. One young couple was so thankful their tiny son arrived safely, they named him *Haruya*, for "Hallelujah"!

Yes, naming the baby is important. Be sure to do it thoughtfully. Remember, that name you choose is for a lifetime.

(Suggested poem to go with this program: "What's in a Name?" in chapter 4. Play a number of the "Name Games," chapter 5.)

THE FINAL WORD

Jesus talks about the joy a woman experiences when she has given birth to a child (John 16:21). She forgets all about the pain of the delivery and the nine months preceding it when she cuddles her newborn baby.

Most mothers experience an emotional "high" when they give birth. There is a feeling of wonder, of accomplishment, of pride, of fulfillment. Sooner or later, however, the new mother is sure to come down to earth from her clouds with a jolt. Maybe it will be when her baby wakes up at 2:00 A.M. and demands to be fed. Maybe it will be when her new baby has colic and screams for several hours during the evening. Maybe it will be when a little one becomes ill, and the new mother doesn't know what to do for him. Maybe it will be when a new mother becomes so weary she feels she cannot care for her baby. Maybe some days everything will go wrong for her. She may even become angry.

God, who made mothers and babies, understands the problems that arise in every family. In His wonderful Book that tells us about important matters, such as how to get rid of our sins and get to heaven, He also gives instructions to new mothers about many practical matters.

Here is a list of verses to read. There is one for every crisis. *(Read verses aloud. Make a copy beforehand to give to the new mother.)* What to read when:

Tired = Matthew 11:28; Psalm 37:7

Weak = Philippians 4:13; Isaiah 40:29

Angry = Psalm 37:8

Worried = Philippians 4:6,7; Matthew 6:31-34

Troubled = John 14:27; Isaiah 43:2

Illness comes = James 5:15; Psalm 103:3

Everything goes wrong = Isaiah 55:8,9; Romans 8:28; 1 Thessalonians 5:18

You don't know what to do = James 1:5; Proverbs 3:5,6

You'll be amazed at how much better things will go for you if you let God have the final word.

DARE WE BRING A BABY INTO TODAY'S WORLD?

Some people fear to have children today because of the state of the world. What about the rising crime rate, increased use of drugs and alcohol, "free love," lawlessness, wars, and pollution?

Mothers and fathers have always had less than ideal conditions in which to rear their children. Think of Jochebed, Moses' mother. She and her husband were oppressed slaves in Egypt. What future was there for their children? They would be slaves, too.

But Jochebed had faith in God. After she gave birth to her baby, she hid him for three months. Then she put him in a little basket in the river and trusted him to God. We know the story—Pharaoh's daughter found him and adopted him as her son, allowing Jochebed to continue caring for him until he was weaned.

God had a wonderful plan for Jochebed's son. He became the great leader of Israel, used of God to deliver the nation from the bondage of Egypt.

God has a great plan for your son or daughter too. Certainly the world is in bad shape. That is all the more reason we should populate it with Christians whom God can use to bring His message to many.

(Name of honoree), we're happy you are having (have had) a baby, and we will pray with you for him (her). We encourage you to trust God for your child as Jochebed did for hers. He will also care for your baby and make him a blessing to many.

Shall we pray now for wisdom for (name of honoree) in bringing up her child to know and love the Savior? (Prayer.)

THE WELCOMED CRISIS

Birth is often spoken of as a blessed event. Truly it is. But it also is a happening that can be rightfully described as a crisis. Feelings closely akin to panic often hit a couple before and after the birth of a child.

In becoming parents, both become aware of the awesome and mysterious nature of life itself. The human individual begins life as a bit of protoplasm smaller than a period at the end of a sentence.

Between fertilization and birth, the human ovum multiplies itself two hundred billion times. Learning about the complex process of human development often arouses feelings of wonder and reverence in a couple. In experiencing the miracle of birth they become aware of the Creator who enables them to participate with Him in the creation of a new life.

Why the panic at such a glorious time? There is so much to learn, to adjust to, to do. Two Bible mothers and their reactions to birth can help us resist pushing the panic button.

(Read 1 Samuel 1:10-11, 20-28.) Hannah wanted a baby desperately. Her pregnancy came about by a prayer miracle. It brought her much joy. Still, her child's birth brought about the same changes that accompany most births. Hannah had to make changes in her life. She was no longer free to come and go as she previously had. Her times with her husband were altered. She could no longer concentrate upon him alone.

We sense in Elkanah a little of the all-too-familiar feeling of jealously new fathers face. Because the baby occupies so much of Mother's time, Dad actually feels he's been left out or replaced in her affection. Still, Elkanah adjusted to not having the pleasure of her company on their annual religious pilgrimage, saying that he desired only that the "Lord confirm His word." Hannah and Elkanah rejoiced together that they had the opportunity to bring a child up for God's service in spite of the adjustments the child brought about.

Mary was a young woman who was surprised at the forthcoming birth of a son. "Panic" could well have been an apt word to describe her emotions as she faced the shame and possible stoning at being pregnant while unmarried. But she accepted the fact as a blessed event and praised God (Read Luke 1:38,49). Little is told us of the adjustments Mary and Joseph had to make at the birth of Jesus, but it must have been a time of crisis.

As with all couples, they faced a change in roles from single adults to parents. They faced a space adjustment—finding a place large enough to accommodate another person. A move to another country to protect the child was even necessary. Mary and Joseph's lives were indeed rearranged when Jesus joined their family.

We can learn from those two mothers to adjust to the changes that a new baby inevitably produces. Prayer and praise are the best antidotes to panic in every circumstance.

ANIMAL BABIES

(This devotional can be separated into several devotional thoughts for use at different showers.)

In the Bible we read, "Now ask the beasts, and let them teach you; and the birds of heaven, and let them tell you" (Job 12:7). What do the beasts and birds teach us about rearing our young?

KANGAROO

A kangaroo is born only one month after he is conceived. He is a helpless, blind, pink mite less than one inch long. Instinct tells him to scramble up into his mother's pouch as soon as he is born, where he will find the nipples to nourish him. The baby kangaroo stays in his mother's pouch for four months before he ventures out into the big wide world. Even then he scurries back when frightened or hungry. By the time he is six months old, however, he has learned to eat grass and leaves like his mother and leaves the pouch to a younger brother or sister. At two years of age he weighs two hundred pounds and is a full-grown kangaroo.

The young kangaroo teaches us the importance of food for growth—spiritual food as well as physical. Babies grow physically when they eat proper food. We grow spiritually when we read God's Word, pray, and fellowship with other believers. The Bible says, "But grow in the grace and knowledge of our Lord and Savior, Jesus Christ" (2 Peter 3:18). We learn from the kangaroo what a difference good nourishment makes—and that goes for spiritual nourishment, too!

BLACK BEAR

Did you know that black bears weigh only eight ounces at birth even though their mothers may weigh three hundred pounds? They have only a thin covering of hair at first and cannot see for the first thirty-five days of their lives.

Mother Bear need not teach her cubs how to swim or climb trees—they are born with that knowledge, just as human babies know how to crawl and then walk without being taught. They do need to be taught how to find food, however, and they need to learn obedience.

The cub's survival depends upon his instant obedience, for the forest is full of danger. The mother bear punishes her cub severely if he disobeys, not because she is cruel, but because she loves him. Black bears teach us something important about child rearing. If we insist on obedience, our "cubs" will be better off, too, in this world with its pitfalls and dangers.

EAGLES

Did you know that eagles mate for life? They also return to the same nest year after year, making necessary repairs and decorating it with bright objects such as light bulbs and fishing plugs. Mr. Bald Eagle is a model husband and father, helping his mate egg-sit during the thirty-five days they must be incubated. He also keeps enemies away from the nest.

As the father and mother eagles bring home food, the scraggly little eaglets eat and grow quickly. Soon they are crawling about their roomy nest (some nests are as large as ten feet across and twenty feet high!) Next they make practice jumps into the air. At thirteen weeks they are ready for a real flight. The father or mother dangles a piece of meat or fish just out of their reach to tempt them to jump out and try their wings.

The eaglet is frightened at first but soon finds himself flying. We push our "eaglets" out of the nest when we send them off to school. They need to try their wings, too, and not be too dependent upon us.

HUMMINGBIRD

God has taught the tiny hummingbird how to make a nest that stretches as her family grows. She uses such materials as cobwebs, caterpillar nests and bits of plant down. As the nest fills with her young, it stretches to make room for them all.

That reminds us that if God cares for the birds of the air, He will also care for us. There are always room and provisions for one more!

KILLDEER

The killdeer protects her young by a clever ruse. God has given her eggs the color of the ground where she hides them. Unless you look very closely, you would think they are lumps of mud. Father Killdeer does his part too. As soon as the eggs hatch, he disposes of the shells that would give enemies a hint of his newborn offspring.

When an enemy approaches the nest, the mother killdeer runs away from the nest, squawks loudly, and drags one wing as if injured. The enemy forgets the young and turns its attention to her. When they are far enough away from the nest, Mother Killdeer stops pretending she is injured and soars into the air.

We do everything we can to protect our children from harm, too, not only physical harm but spiritual as well. We cannot start too soon to tell our babies about the Savior who loves and cares for them.

ANIMAL BABYSITTERS

There are babysitters in the animal world as well as in the human world. Penguins in Antarctica leave their partially grown young in the care of a few old birds while they go fishing. Ducks also take turns babysitting for one another. Lion fathers are not much help after their offspring are born—Dad takes off. Mother Lion does not dare leave her cubs alone in the lair because of the dangers of hyenas, wild dogs, eagles, ants, or people who might harm them. She arranges to live with another female lion who has the same problem as she. One "cat sits" while the other one looks for food. If the wild beasts can cooperate to find solutions to their problems, we should be able to as well.

GREAT GRANDMAS

Who can measure the influence of a godly grandmother? Or an ungodly one? Jezebel was one of the latter. That princess of Sidon, who married King Ahab, introduced immoral Baal worship to Israel, causing the people to turn away from God and turn to sin.

Jezebel's evil influence reached even beyond Israel. Her daughter married the son of godly King Jehoshaphat of Judah and became the queen of that realm when her husband became king. We read of King Jehoram: "And he walked in the way of the kings of Israel, just as the house of Ahab did (for Ahab's [and Jezebel's] daughter was his wife), and he did evil in the sight of the LORD" (2 Chronicles 21:6).

When King Jehoram died, after a wicked and stormy reign, his son Ahaziah became king. "He also walked in the ways of the house of Ahab for his mother was his counselor to do wickedly" (2 Chronicles 22:3). Like mother, like daughter, like grandson. So our influence spreads from one generation to another.

What a difference a godly grandmother makes. Paul said to Timothy, who was his son in the faith: "I am mindful of the sincere faith within you, which first dwelt in your grandmother Lois, and your mother Eunice, and I am sure that it is in you as well" (2 Timothy 1:5). Paul did not say anything about Timothy's grandfather or father; they may have been unbelievers. But his godly grandmother's influence led him to become a believer and Paul's successor.

Perhaps it was Grandmother Lois who taught Timothy the Scriptures that he learned as a child and that made such a difference in his life (2 Timothy 3:15).

Mike Warnke, author of the book *The Satan Sellers* tells in his testimony of his grandmother, who never gave up praying for him even when he had become involved in drugs and Satan worship. "If you have a little white-haired grandma praying for you," he wrote, "you may as well give up. Her prayers are going to be answered!"

You may be neither old nor white-haired, but as a grandmother you exert a tremendous influence upon your children, your grandchildren, and your great grandchildren. The godly life of a Christian grandmother will go down through the generations as an example for her descendants to follow. Her prayers will reach through the years and through the tears to bring Christ and His blessings to her offspring and to others as well.

Grandmother, God is giving *(or has given)* you a precious grandchild for you to love and pray for. Your faithfulness will be rewarded and your prayers answered with blessings upon your offspring. God bless you!

(If possible, give this devotional in your own words rather than reading it.)

4

Poems—Words Fitly Spoken

Some of the following poems have lovely devotional thoughts to help a new mother center her thoughts upon God. Others are humorous. All are designed to say just what you wanted to say but could not find the right words.

Thinking of Baby

Baby awake is a mischievous elf
Who can keep you busy
In spite of yourself!
A rollicking, frolicking,
    gurgling sprite
Who may sleep half the day . . .
(And cry half the night!)

But yet when you're humming
    a last lullaby,
And the sandman has come
And closed each little eye . . .
Gone is the elf, and you find
    out instead,
You've just tucked a tired
    little angel in bed.

Author Unknown

Ten Commandments for Parents

1. Take your child to Sunday School and church, and teach him God's Word at home.
2. Lead your child into a personal faith in Jesus Christ.
3. Give your child the support of your love and confidence.
4. Plan to do fun things with your child, trying to see things from his viewpoint.
5. Teach your child the value and joy of work by giving him a share in the household tasks.
6. Be consistent in the discipline of your child, punishing him for wrongdoing even when you're not in the mood.
7. Be generous with praise and sparing with criticism.
8. Teach your child that obstacles can be changed into opportunities.
9. Be an example for your children to follow.
10. Make your home a center of friendliness for neighbors and friends.

Children Learn What They Live

If a child lives with criticism, he learns to condemn.
If a child lives with hostility, he learns to fight.
If a child lives with ridicule, he learns to be shy.
If a child lives with shame, he learns to feel guilty.
If a child lives with tolerance, he learns to be patient.
If a child lives with encouragement, he learns confidence.
If a child lives with praise, he learns to appreciate.
If a child lives with fairness, he learns justice.
If a child lives with security, he learns to have faith.
If a child lives with approval, he learns to like himself.
If a child lives with acceptance and friendship, he learns to find love in the world.

Dorothy Law Nolte

Boy or Girl?

Some folks pray for a boy, and some
　　For a golden-haired little girl to come.
Some claim to think there is more of joy
　　Wrapped up in the smile of a little boy,
While others pretend that the silky curls
　　And plump, pink cheeks of the little girls
Bring more of bliss to the old home place
　　Than a small boy's queer little freckled face.

Now which is better, I couldn't say
　　If the Lord should ask me to choose today;
If He should put in a call for me
　　And say: "Now what shall your order be,
A boy or girl? I have both in store —
　　Which of the two are you waiting for?"
I'd say with one of my broadest grins:
　　"Send either one, if it can't be twins."

I've heard it said, to some people's shame,
　　They cried with grief when a small boy came.
For they wanted a girl. And some folks I know
　　Who wanted a boy, just took on so
When a girl was sent. But it seems to me
　　That mothers and fathers should happy be
To think, when the Stork has come and gone,
　　That the Lord would trust them with either one.

Boy or girl? There can be no choice;
　　There's something lovely in either voice.
And all that I ask of the Lord to do
　　Is to see that the mother comes safely through.
And guard the baby and have it well, with a perfect form and a
　　　　　　　healthy yell,

And a pair of eyes and a shock of hair.
Then, boy or girl—and its dad won't care.

Edgar A. Guest

To a Child Asleep

Little daughter, wearing silver moonbeams in your hair,
    Shadow babies playing hide-and-seek across your dimpled
        face,
You cannot hear the prayer my heart would make for you
    As I sit quietly in your darkened room.
I would not ask that you be beautiful of face or form,
    Nor that you wear the weary world's bright toothpaste smile.
I only pray that you have true beauty which is love,
    That from the fountain of your soul may flow
        an endless stream of it
To quench the thirst of all who need you.
I do not ask that you be clever, dear, nor witty-wise,
    But that your wisdom may be that which plumbs th'eternal
        mines
    Of Truth, and rediscovers gems of Faith and Loyalty and
        Hope.
I do not wish for fame for you, my child, for Fame
    Is fickle; she gives her favors indiscriminately and
        tomorrow passes on.
If you must suffer, let it make you strong, refine you
    And let it usher you into the presence of the Author of all
        life.

Of you, He'll mold a volume of great worth and blessing.
And when "Finis" is written to your life, its pages will be
bound in gold.
If God sees fit to heed my prayer, you'll live abundantly—
And you'll be a woman, my daughter.

Ann Washburn Davis

From *The Sunday School Builder*, May 1960. Copyright 1960, The Sunday School Board of the Southern Baptist Convention. All rights reserved. Used by permission.

The Ravages of Time

He's handsome, He's engaged, He uses "Brut!"
There's no lint and no speck on his tailor-made suit.
The lovely young thing clinging to his arm
Just radiates grace and bride-to-be charm.
With mutual scorn they view a tired mother
Herding to church three kids and new brother,
Whose husband follows with diapers and purse,
His wedding suit sagging from awful to worse.
The groom-to-be swears he'll never be slack—
When he's a new father, he'll still keep his knack.
And the bride-to-be vows, one way or another
She'll ne'er be so frazzled when she's a young mother.

But the years have passed since they said, "I do,"
And they've another baby for all to view.
There's the proud Poppa in his tailor-made suit,
Now speckled with lint and not smelling of "Brut."
The crease is now gone and there in its stead
Is the burped-up-trail from that new curly-head.
The sweet young thing now walks in the fore
With a wiggly bundle who just burped some more.

Her hair is limp, her tone is terse
And tagging behind is the brute with the purse.

Betty Jo Mathis

From Betty Jo Mathis, Common to Man (La Grange, Wyoming: Mathis, 1969). Used by permission.

Spit Baths

Of all the curses known to youth
(I tell you this in somber truth)
There's none that ever could be worse
than having Mom reach in her purse,
Take out her hanky, start her search,
And give us spit baths on the way to church.

At home our dad has guaranteed
that all us boys are clean, indeed.
He's checked us all with manly skill,
and we're all satisfied—until
Our Mom begins her sputt-ring search,
and we get spit baths on the way to church!

Oh, would some pow'r us deliver
when Dad starts up the fam'ly flivver,
And we're all dressed in Sunday best
and Mom begins her weekly quest,
Attacking while we yelp and lurch,
bestowing spit baths on the way to church!

I'll have you know, when I'm a Dad
    and all my boys are Sunday-clad,
E'en tho' they're smeared with jam or hash
    and have a milky-way mustache,
I'll make my wife just keep her perch—
    there'll be no spit-baths on the way to church!

Betty Jo Mathis

No Boys—No Fun

The tho't, it comes to me, How simple life would be,
    How neat, how free from noise, If there were no little
boys.
No sun-burned, toothless guys, with mischief in their eyes,
    In wrong-side-out T-shirts, to track in dust and dirt.
No need for Mom to fume, at cluttered, junk-strewn room;
    No sox in crazy places, shoes with frazzled laces.
No dirty underwear beneath the comp'ny chair,
    No frenzied schoolbook search, No unzipped pants in
    church.
No pets, no bugs, no pups, no busted china cups.
    No deaf'ning shout, "We won!" No noise, no boys, no
fun!

Betty Jo Mathis

"Spit Baths" and "No Boys—No Fun" are from Betty Jo Mathis, *Of Throne and Footstool* (LaGrange, Wyoming: Mathis, 1972), and are used by permission.

A Mother's Prayer

He's such a little fellow, Lord,
   but oh, I thank Thee for him.
I thank Thee for bringing us through our Valley
   and then on this Mountain top.
Help me to walk worthy of all Thy blessings.
He lay so long beneath my heart, and now as I hold him
   in my arms—he's such a "bundle of possibilities,"
this flesh of my flesh and bone of my bone.
   My heart cries out for wisdom!
Lord, give me patience and understanding with this little one,
               and as his inquisitive little mind
   brings him into corners of the home now sacred to others,
help me to wisely channel him into places that his little world
               can understand.
And as I watch as he fills his pockets with little treasures that
               only a boy could prize—
   a pretty stone, a piece of string, a broken knife, a bit of this-
               or-that,
O Lord, may I, in Thy strength, learn to fill his mind
   and heart with wisdom from Thee.
May he learn to love all mankind in this world of unrest and
   hate.
Lord, lead me, give me an abundance of wisdom, this is my daily
   prayer.
For without Thee I am nothing, and this little being,
   this miracle of Love, could not be.
This is a holy and wonderful and awesome responsibility
   You have given me, Lord, to mold a character.
Help me to face up to the task ahead, and when I falter—and
   fail—help me to pick myself up and try again.
For a mother's job is a never ending one.
Yes, Lord, give me patience and understanding and wisdom.
Lord, lead me.

                              Florence Anderson

41

Postpartum Blues

According to old Doctor Spock a brand new mom should not be shocked
To find when baby's still quite new, she gets a case of weepy blues.
Postpartum blues is what they're dubbed—a time when Mama feels she's flubbed
And wonders why she did conceive and if success she will achieve.
For once the babe is seen by all, the relatives both great and small,
The mama new is then beset with views and notions from Aunt Het.
And cousin Jane and Gramma Jones who pat the child and feel his bones,
Give advice for every issue—cradle cap to toilet tissue.
No paragoric!? No belly bands!? And fed whenever he demands??
Orange juice will give him pimples—tickling feet will make him simple.
Guard his soft spot—watch his navel (So says second cousin, Ravel.)
Grand Dad says those things don't matter—what he needs is to be fatter!
And so they come and give their views and that provokes postpartum blues!
But little mother, do not fear all the tales that you will hear;
Just tell those relatives and gents that you were born with Mother-sense.
That child is yours, and you're quite bright, so tell the kin to fly a kite!

Betty Jo Mathis

From Betty Jo Mathis, *Dinner of Herbs* (LaGrange, Wyoming: Mathis, 1975). Used by permission.

What Might Have Been

"The hand that rocks the cradle"—but today there's no such
hand.
It's bad to rock the baby, they would have us understand;
So the cradle's but a relic of the former foolish days,
When mothers reared their children in unscientific ways;
When they jounced them and they bounced them, those poor
dwarfs of long ago—
The Washingtons and Jeffersons and Adamses, you know.

William Croswell Doane

Hand in Hand

She placed her hand in mine
Pudgy, tender, and small—
Expecting that the size of my hand
Might prevent a serious fall.

She yielded her life to my guidance—
Trusting, depending, and sure—
That whatever the plight or danger
With me she would be secure.

The responsibility O Lord is frightening!
To have a task so divine!
For assurance of the right direction,
Let me place my hand in thine.
James C. Barry

From *Living With Children*, Oct.-Dec. 1958. Copyright 1958, The Sunday
School Board of the Southern Baptist Convention. All rights reserved. Used
by permission.

To An Adopted Child

Not flesh of my flesh
   Not bone of my bone
But still miraculously my own
   Never forget
     For a single minute
You didn't grow under my heart
   But in it.
            Author Unknown

All On Account of the Baby

An ache in the back and an ache in the arms,
   All on account of the baby.
A fear and a fright and a thousand alarms,
   All on account of the baby.
And bottles and rattles and whistles and rings,
   From cellar to attic a clutter of things,
From morning to night and to morning again
   More fuss and more fume than an army of men,
And a head that is stupid for lack of its sleep,
   And a heart where a flood of anxieties leap—
All on account of the baby.

A joy in the heart and a light in the eyes,
   All on account of the baby.
A growing content and a growing surprise,
   All on account of the baby.
And patience that conquers a myriad frets,
   And a sunshiny song that another begets,
And pureness of soul as a baby is pure,
   And sureness of faith as the children are sure,

And a glory of love between husband and wife,
And a saner and happier outlook on life,
All on account of the baby.

Amos R. Wells

Adult Education

You don't have to go to college to get an education
Nor must you write a term-page or a lengthy dissertation
If you are seeking to be wise, you can skip the PhD.
Just get yourself a partner and raise a family.
No books perused within the finest ivy halls
Can impart the lessons one can learn within his own four walls.
This school is open nite and day, with teachers young but wise
Revealing texts anew each day to those with open eyes.
The lessons learned within the home are not for mind apart
But for training of the inner man, to cultivate the heart.
The subjects, they are varied—offering many courses
And the questions to be answered stem from strangest sources.
Classes in humility and honesty are taught—
Truths that some have never learned, but wisest men have
    sought.

Biology, Geology, Linguistics and more
Are taught by lisping bug collectors, displaying all their lore.
Applied Psychology too, this institute will bring—
Taught to you unwittingly by your very own offspring.
Some lessons here are only learned thru' tears and bitter strife
And answers often not revealed 'til later on in life.
The scholars, tho' they're parents, are frequently so slow
And must be taught repeatedly the truths they need to know.
But the tutors are forgiving, teaching you the same—
Quick to forget the errors, nor holding one to blame.
The tuition, true is costly, in stress and anxious fears

But returns are more than ample as you ponder on the years
And see your masters, grown mature, to view with mellowed eyes
And honor you, cum laude, and count you with the wise.

Betty Jo Mathis

From Betty Jo Mathis, Common to Man (LaGrange, Wyoming: Mathis, 1969).
Used by permission.

What's In a Name?

When I look over my family tree
    The strangest assortment of titles I see
Names such as Hartford, Irving, Ceola
    Aubrey and Cleo, Gershom, Etola.

And I can't help having my doubts and my "maybes"
    (Didn't my ancestors like little babies?)
Why burden a newborn, so sweet and so tiny
    With a name like Myrtle, Minnie or Miny?

Can you just imagine burping an Emer,
    Or cuddling a Wilbur when he was a screamer?
What did it do to their ego, their id
    To grow up with a handle like Cleburn or Thid?

And what of my Grandma, who was called Lilly Bruce
    Did a name such as that become common with use?
Or her sisters, who were Fannie, Sadie and Hattie—
    Has Great Grandma not heard of Debbie or Patty?

But I s'pose as time goes marching on
    And in the year two-thousand-fifty-one,
Names we like now will then sound odd—
    Such as Mike and Jack and Craig and Todd.

Can't you just picture a wrinkled Aunt Vicki,
Or tottering and feeble, old Uncle Ricky—
A grandma named Tammy, Jody or Sandy-
A rocking-chair grandad whose first name is Randy
Surrounded by babies, chubby and fat
Named Archibald, Zora and Je-hosh-a-phat!
Betty Jo Mathis

Funniest Thing!

Proud Grandpa went to view
The babies pink and new
Arranged in squalling groups,
Cocoons in sterile coops.
He judged them there en masse,
His nose against the glass
And came with strange report,
"They're all a homely sort
Save one red wrinkled tot,
The choicest of the lot;
And it's plain for all to see—
That one's akin to me!"
Betty Jo Mathis

How Do You Tell a Gramma When You See One?

How do you know she's a gramma? She looks too young for that!
She hasn't got a speck of gray, she's not the least bit fat.
Oh, I know she's a gramma, tho' she doesn't look the part,
I can see it plainly in her ways and know she's one at heart.
Have you not heard her catch her breath when little ones get
    spanked,

Or how she often overlooks a childish lack of thanks?
She trims the bread in tidy squares for one who can't stand
    crusts,
And says it matters not a bit when floors get tracked with dust.
She winks at lots of little pranks her own kids used to pull
That got them into trouble when she held to stricter rule.
She never seems too busy now to hear of youthful feats,
Nor does she seem to mind at all if stories are repeats.
You can't always tell the grammas by looks or height or weight.
They're known by smiles, not styles and *by the stuff they tolerate!*

Betty Jo Mathis

"Funniest Thing" and "How Do You Tell a Gramma When You See One" are
from Betty Jo Mathis, *Dinner of Herbs* (LaGrange, Wyoming: Mathis, 1975),
and are used by permission.

The Stork Club

We thought we'd chased that stork away
    But now we see he's here to stay,
He flits from one house to another
    Leaving a flustered Dad and Mother
He visits the rich—he visits the poor
    He's sure there's always room for more.
He has no respect for age or youth—
    Today it's Sarah—Tomorrow it's Ruth.

Our walls are bulging—our cars are loaded
    It's obvious our population's exploded.
Don't get us wrong—or mistake our emotions
    We just hadn't planned on so many explosions!
That guilty stork now smugly waits
    Atop our roof—just 'biding his date.

But don't you raise your brows nor be sore vexed
And don't you laugh—cause you may be next!
Betty Jo Mathis

"What's In a Name" and "The Stork Club" are from Betty Jo Mathis, *Common to Man* (LaGrange, Wyoming: Mathis, 1969), and are used by permission.

5
Fun and Games

What will you do at your shower? How about playing a few games? Some of the following are new, some old, but all are guaranteed to be fun.

GET ACQUAINTED GAMES

Do all the guests know each other? If not, give each a name tag shaped like a small umbrella. Make a larger upside down paper umbrella for the honoree with drawings of baby gifts in it. Ladies will become better acquainted as they mix while playing the following games.

WHAT DOES BABY SAY?

Find pictures of babies in magazines, mount on colored paper, number and display in the room where the shower is held. Give each guest a piece of paper. Have them look at the pictures and write a caption for each on their papers. What do they imagine the baby would be saying if he could talk? Give a prize for the cleverest captions.

BABY PRODUCTS

Cut out advertisements of baby products from magazines, but eliminate the brand names. Post the numbered advertisements on the wall. Guests will number their papers and wander around "shopping." The guest who figures out the correct brand names first wins the prize. An appropriate prize would be a box containing some miniatures of the products pictured.

WHO AM I?

Write the following names of famous children on pieces of paper and pin on the backs of the guests as they arrive. Instruct them to ask questions that can be answered with "yes" or "no" to find out who they are, such as: "Am I in the Bible?" "Am I a fictitious character?" "Am I living today?"

1. Moses
2. Shirley Temple
3. Christopher Robin
4. Joseph
5. The Gerber baby
6. Laura Ingalls
7. John the Baptist
8. Dennis the Menace
9. Samuel
10. David
11. Linus
12. Benjamin
13. Tom Sawyer
14. Alice in Wonderland

WHOSE CHILD IS THIS?

Have about ten people each bring a picture of one of their babies to the shower, and ask the honoree to bring a baby picture of her husband. Number the pictures and pass around to the ladies. Haven them write on numbered slips of paper whom they think the baby belongs to. The one who gets the greatest number of them correct wins. A fitting gift could be a small photo "brag" album.

TELEGRAM GAME

Instruct each guest to write the name of the honoree across the top of a piece of paper. For instance: MARY SMITH. Now they must write a telegram regarding the birth of her baby using words beginning with the letters of the name, such as, "M̲ary a̲nd r̲obust y̲oung s̲on m̲arching i̲n t̲o h̲ome."

BABY'S FUTURE OCCUPATION

Babysitter?		Fisherman?
Government Job?		Musician?
Farmer?		Florist, Gardener?
	(Paste a baby picture here)	
Banker?		Haberdasher?
Jeweler?	Cowboy?	Fireman?

Make a large poster as illustrated.

Give each player an envelope containing swatches of material to match with the above occupations. Provide paper and pencils to write their findings.

Babysitter—flannel
Government—red bias tape
Farmer—grosgrain ribbon
Banker—small checked material
Fisherman—net
Musician—corduroy
Florist, Gardener—flowered
Haberdasher—felt
Jeweler—material with diamond-shaped pattern
Cowboy—cowboy design
Fireman—nylon hose

You might find material that would suggest other occupations.

DRAW MOTHER-TO-BE

Give each guest a piece of paper and a pencil. Instruct guests to put the paper on top of their heads and draw a picture of the new mother on her way to the hospital in a car. Or turn out the lights and let them draw on their laps. This is a good icebreaker.

GRANDMOTHER GAME

Divide your guests into teams and let them work together to find as many things as possible that a grandmother does as well as words to describe a grandmother, beginning with the letters of GRANDMOTHER. For example, she: G-gives, gushes; R-reminisces, raves.

So to Speak

The parts of speech come into play as guests use adjectives, verbs, adverbs, and rhymes to speak about the "blessed event" in the following games.

STORY WRITTEN BY GUESTS

When the guests arrive, have them sign a guest list so that you have each one's name. Use the following story or write one that suits your situation better. Have each guest give an adjective. Go around more than once if necessary to get enough words. Fill in the story blanks in the order the adjectives are given, then read the completed story aloud. Encourage them to use a variety of adjectives; "stupendous," "gracious," or "heroic" as well as "bland," "sloppy," or "scatterbrained" for more fun. Each adjective may be used only once. Be very careful to switch names or adjectives if in danger of hurting someone who is sensitive.

The _____ gals of the (*name of church, club or community*) decided to have a _____ shower for _____ _____ (*name of honoree*), since she is expecting (*or has had*) a _____ baby. _____ _____ (*name*) and _____ _____ (*name*) planned some _____ games. _____ _____ (*name*) and _____ _____ (*name*) decided upon the _____ refreshments. _____ _____ (*name*) volun-

teered her _____ home for the _____ occasion. Guests
were: (*List all the other guests with blanks in front of their names. Be
sure to include everyone.*) The _____ _____ (*name of
honoree*) was delighted with the _____ gifts given to her by
her _____ friends. Everybody had a _____ time. Best
wishes from all to the _____ baby and her _____
mother. (*This can be varied to suit your situation.*)

WHAT DOES BABY NEED?

Rhyme Time: Find a synonym for each word on the left. The
item Baby needs rhymes with the synonym. Sample: Perhaps = Maybe; *Baby*.
1. A fight
2. Kind of cloth
3. Part of a car
4. Storage place
5. Kind of weather
6. Direction
7. Heavenly body
8. Explosive device
9. Big spoon
10. Kind of bird
Answers: Fight = battle; *rattle*
Kind of cloth = silk; *milk*
Part of a car = bumper; *jumper*
Storage place = bin; *pin*
Kind of weather = muggy; *buggy*
Direction = down; *gown*
Heavenly body = moon; *spoon*
Explosive device = bomb; *mom*
Big spoon = ladle; *cradle*
Kind of bird = dove; *love*

WHAT BABY IS MADE OF

Type on rattles made from construction paper:*

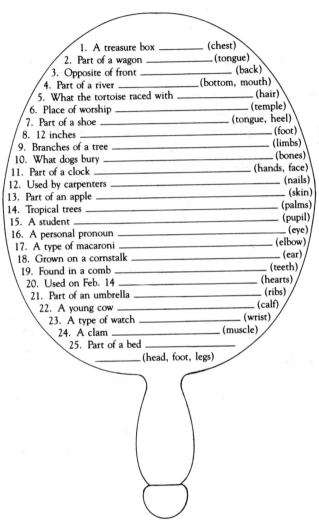

1. A treasure box _____ (chest)
2. Part of a wagon _____ (tongue)
3. Opposite of front _____ (back)
4. Part of a river _____ (bottom, mouth)
5. What the tortoise raced with _____ (hair)
6. Place of worship _____ (temple)
7. Part of a shoe _____ (tongue, heel)
8. 12 inches _____ (foot)
9. Branches of a tree _____ (limbs)
10. What dogs bury _____ (bones)
11. Part of a clock _____ (hands, face)
12. Used by carpenters _____ (nails)
13. Part of an apple _____ (skin)
14. Tropical trees _____ (palms)
15. A student _____ (pupil)
16. A personal pronoun _____ (eye)
17. A type of macaroni _____ (elbow)
18. Grown on a cornstalk _____ (ear)
19. Found in a comb _____ (teeth)
20. Used on Feb. 14 _____ (hearts)
21. Part of an umbrella _____ (ribs)
22. A young cow _____ (calf)
23. A type of watch _____ (wrist)
24. A clam _____ (muscle)
25. Part of a bed _____
_____ (head, foot, legs)

*To save time, trace around the shape several times on a sheet of construction paper, using up to five carbons. Type before cutting out.

A BOUQUET FOR BABY

Fill in the blanks with names of flowers.
1. You might name a girl baby _____ (Rose, Violet, or Daisy).
2. You give your baby to drink _____ (Carnation).
3. He wakes up for his feeding at _____ (Four O'clock).
4. Brings Grandma running _____ (Baby tears).
5. Affectionate name for Dad _____ (Poppy).
6. Sweetest smell on earth is _____ (Baby's breath).
7. Color of cheeks _____ (Pinks, Rose).
8. What baby kisses you with _____ (Tulips).
9. How Grandpa acts when Baby is naughty _____ (Mum).
10. You might name a baby boy _____ (Sweet William).

ANIMAL BABIES

Test your zoological knowledge with this game to name the animal babies. Write the baby names beside the adult animal name. Can you name them all in five minutes?

1. Bear _____ (cub)
2. Horse _____ (colt)
3. Buffalo _____ (calf)
4. Duck _____ (duckling)
5. Tiger _____ (kitten, cub)
6. Fox _____ (kit, cub)
7. Hen _____ (pullet)
8. Swine _____ (piglet)
9. Cat _____ (kitten)
10. Frog _____ (polliwog)
11. Sheep _____ (lamb)
12. Cow _____ (calf)
13. Dog _____ (puppy)
14. Deer _____ (fawn)
15. Elephant _____ (calf)
16. Chicken _____ (chicks)
17. Goose _____ (gosling)
18. Lion _____ (cub)
19. Seal _____ (calf)
20. Bull _____ (bullock)

DOUBLE-TALK

Each phrase below suggests an idea that has to do with two.
1. An old Spanish gold coin   (doubloon)
2. A swindle   (double-cross)

3. A flower	(tulip)
4. Slang for a coin	(two-bit piece)
5. A popular marriage rite	(double-ring ceremony)
6. A fruit	(pear)
7. A very short poem	(couplet)
8. Cooking pans	(double boiler)
9. A coat with two rows of buttons	(double-breasted)
10. A baseball term	(doubleheader, double play)

An appropriate prize for the winner would be a pair of salt and pepper shakers.

BABY DARLING

Give each guest (or couple) a slip of paper and pencil. Instruct guests to spell out BABY DARLING down the left-hand side of the paper. Each guest or couple should then think of adjectives describing Baby Darling, beginning with those letters: bald, adorable, and so on. Have the one who finishes first read her list and give her a prize of safety pins or some other baby object, which she in turn will give to the honoree. Then have the guests write *verbs* beginning with the same letters: bounces, aggravates, and others.

You can also do this with the words MOTHER and FATHER.

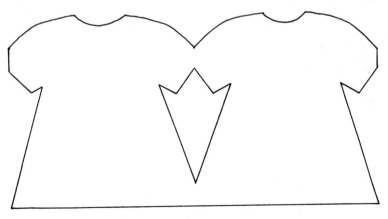

LITTLE STRANGER

Fold a sheet of pastel colored paper in half lengthwise and cut out a double baby dress as illustrated. Print LITTLE on the left side and STRANGER on the right as acrostics. Party participants will list articles beginning with each letter that the little stranger will need. The first one who finishes wins.

Name Games

It's fun to help name the new baby. Several games give guests this privilege.

ACROSTICS

Cut out bootee shapes like the pattern shown. On each, print acrostic fashion the father's and mother's first names. Ask each guest to think up as many names for boys beginning with the letters of the father's name as possible, and to think up girl names beginning with the letters in the mother's name. A variation would be to write in acrostic fashion "Baby Jones," (parents' last name) and beside each letter write a suggested name beginning with that letter.

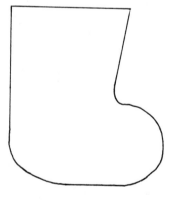

Divide into pairs. Assign each pair one of the following names and have them pantomine the first part until the others guess the name.

Keith—a key
Barbara—a barb
Mary—a mare
Matthew—a mat
Walter—a wall

Richard—rich
Lois—low
Harriet—hair
Henrietta—a hen
Robert—rob

WHO'S WHO?

What names do these clues suggest to you? Several have more than one right answer.

Boys' Names

1. A private investigator (Dick)
2. An implement used to change a tire (Jack)
3. Comes due every month (Bill)
4. A man of nobility (Don, Earl)
5. For moving (Van)
6. Comes from the sun (Ray)
7. A winner (Victor)
8. A weapon (Lance)
9. The good guy in cowboy film (Marshal)
10. Radio operators' slang (Roger)
11. Sincere (Frank, Ernest)
12. A permanent wave (Tony)

Girls' Names

1. Goes ding-dong (Belle)
2. A jewel (Pearl, Ruby, Opal)
3. Exuberant, happy (Joy)
4. A green fruit (Olive)
5. Just a nut! (Hazel)
6. A part of the eyes (Iris)
7. A southern state (Georgia, Virginia)
8. Blowing up a storm (Gale)
9. Heavenly body (Venus, Star)
10. Thanks at mealtime (Grace)
11. A flower (Rose, Daisy)
12. A climbing vine (Ivy)

BIBLE NAMES

Shower guests list their favorite Bible names for the honoree as character references. Each tells why she thinks that Bible character was an admirable person.

TWIN NAMES

Help the mother-to-be by suggesting good names for twins. Hers may be a double blessing. Write those on the bootee and give it to the honoree for future reference.

Variation: Hold a relay patterned after a spelling bee. Line the guests up in two teams opposite each other. The first person on a team calls out a name. Her opponent opposite her on the other team must give a twin name in ten seconds or drop out. The winner will be the last contestant standing. Choose a fast writer to list the good matches to give to the honoree.

SCRAMBLED DICKS AND DORAS

Give each player a copy of the following scrambled names. A prize goes to the one with the most correct answers in the shortest length of time.

Boys' Names	Girls' Names
1. HDCA—(Chad)	1. LYOHL—(Holly)
2. NYAR—(Ryan)	2. TEANENT—(Annette)
3. HIMLECA—(Michael)	3. LEMLICHE—(Michelle)
4. DTDO—(Todd)	4. AYRM—(Mary)
5. EJYEMR—(Jeremy)	5. RJINENFE—(Jennifer)
6. THANNA—(Nathan)	6. NLYN—(Lynn)
7. KARTIPC—(Patrick)	7. ARSHA—(Sarah)
8. LADDON—(Donald)	8. PSTAINEEH—(Stephanie)
9. CIER—(Eric)	9. THUR—(Ruth)
10. NSAJO—(Jason)	10. TYACRSL—(Crystal)
11. YDARN—(Randy)	11. IREULA—(Laurie)
12. THEEBRR—(Herbert)	12. NOCNEI—(Connie)

NAME HUNT

On bib-shaped construction paper like the one outlined, type the following strange-sounding sentences. Hidden within the sentences are many names that could be chosen for the new baby. Circle or underline the names. The player who finds the most names wins the prize.

NAME HUNT
Find the hidden names in these sentences.
There are at least thirty names, depending on spelling.

1. Don't let the vapor mar your smart hat.
2. Never a plumber that works all year.
3. He skates in the final ice tournament.
4. The roosters strut half the length of the lane.
5. If you sand raw lumber nicely it will be easy to decorate.
6. It may be that no lives were lost in the big race.
7. Something about them made us test her cake and in a hurry.
8. Tell Engineer Jones to have her sing the carol in English.
9. He had a plan to audit his own issue annually.
10. She donned a darling dress and ran downstairs.

MERRY MIX-UPS

Scrambled word games to "rattle" your brain!

WHAT TO EXPECT

From a Baby:
1. EWT OMTOTBS _____ (wet bottoms)
2. YITRD APIDRES _____ (dirty diapers)
3. PUCCHIS _____ (hiccups)
4. KITCSY KSISSE _____ (sticky kisses)
5. YBAB KATL _____ (baby talk)

From Little Girls:
1. SELFFUR & SNBOBIR _____ (ruffles and ribbons)
2. DSESIH & SLLOD _____ (dishes and dolls)
3. PMIPRGIN _____ (primping)
4. CUSIM SNOLSSE _____ (music lessons)
5. LGIGINGG _____ (giggling)

From Little Boys:
1. SUBG & GROFS _____ (bugs and frogs)
2. SMURD & RONSH _____ (drums and horns)
3. WOCSBOY & DANNIIS _____ (cowboys and Indians)
4. RDYTI DAHSN _____ (dirty hands)
5. LTAL SATLE _____ (tall tales)

WHAT BABY NEEDS

ribc	(crib)
tletar	(rattle)
ibb	(bib)
apc	(cap)
wong	(gown)
otletb	(bottle)
grevcieni tankleb	(receiving blanket)
inps	(pins)
rdieap	(diaper)
nobnet	(bonnet)
rihst	(shirt)
dowerp	(powder)
facpiire	(pacifier)
sansibet	(bassinet)
tfanin atse	(infant seat)
slapcit snatp	(plastic pants)
tnooil	(lotion)
atvisnmi	(vitamins)
ahri shrub	(hair brush)
reetdn glivno reca	(tender loving care)

THE NOSE KNOWS

THIS IS BABY'S NOSE

Players sit in a circle with a leader, who holds a doll. The leader stands before a player, points to some part of the doll's body, and calls it by the name of some other part. The player addressed must point to the part of his own body mentioned by the leader, but he must *call* it the part to which the leader pointed. For instance, the leader may say, pointing to the doll's foot, "This is baby's nose." She then counts to ten. If the player to whom she is speaking does not point to his *nose* and say, "This is baby's foot," before ten is counted, she becomes the next leader.

UMMM-GOOD

Invite guests to use their noses to discern what to feed the baby. Number small dishes of several kinds of baby food. Ask guests to smell, with eyes blindfolded, each dish and by its corresponding number list what they think the food is. The prize? Several jars of baby food!

A TASTY TEST

The senses of smell and taste are closely related, especially in this game. Prepare glasses containing several liquids of distinctive tastes that baby may drink. Place a number on each glass. Players will sip from separate straws a little taste of the liquids and then identify it. To make sure this is a test of the nose and tongue, blindfold each player before she tastes the liquid so the appearance of the liquid will not give her a clue. Some suitable liquids are: milk, water, orange juice, apple juice, apple pineapple juice, prune orange juice, and so on. Reward the winner with a can of juice.

GOOD TO THE LAST DROP

Have you some really good sports? Or could you pick on a couple of guys for this strictly-for-fun game? Prepare two baby bottles filled with Seven-Up for this contest. Enlarge the holes in the nipples to make the game move more quickly. Ask the two contestants to sit back-to-back in the middle of the guests. They are to race to see who can empty his bottle first. Declare the winner the town's "Biggest Sucker"!

The Braille System

The hands get in on the act in these games.

PORTRAITS

We all like to predict who the baby will resemble. Each will make her prediction by holding a piece of paper behind her back and tearing it to resemble a baby. These "portraits" are given to the honoree to judge the one she thinks looks most like her expected one. (Hint: It helps to make a more recognizable baby if the guests fold their papers before tearing them.)

DIAPERING IN THE DARK

Remind the new mother that she will soon discover babies have to be changed in the dark of night. You want to help her learn how to take care of this task without turning on all the lights and waking up her hubby. To discover who can best teach her how to diaper by the Braille system, each lady will take her turn diapering a doll while blindfolded. Time each contestant. The winner receives the honor of being invited to the honoree's house to help with 2:00 A.M. changings!

HOW DO YOU FEEL?

Finding the proper things to care for other needs of the baby during those wee hours calls for hands skilled to the touch. See who can recognize and remember the most articles felt on a tray or in a bag while blindfolded or with eyes closed. Tell them the number of articles useful for baby in the container and let them write what they remember after all have felt. A clever prize for the winner might be a night light for the nursery!

CHARADES

You'll be surprised at how many good actresses you have in your group!

WHAT ARE THEY DOING?

Assign the following to several individuals to pantomime while the others guess what they are doing. Explain that it all has to do with the new baby coming.
1. Nervous father in hospital waiting room.
2. Grandma seeing first grandchild.
3. Tired mother getting up at night to feed baby.
4. New father changing the baby.
5. Mother feeding baby his first cereal.

NURSERY RHYMES

Write familiar nursery rhymes on paper bootees. Have individuals or groups pantomime the rhymes while others guess. (Mary had a little lamb, Jack be nimble, This little pig, Hickory dickory dock, There was an old woman, and so on.)

For variation, divide into two groups. Each group selects a list of nursery rhymes for representatives from the other group to illustrate on chalkboard or large paper for their own team to guess. Allow only sixty seconds for the drawing.

6

Fancy Fixin's

Decorating for your shower is worth all the extra time it takes to make more memorable the parties to welcome wee ones into God's wonderful world. These can be beautiful whether simple or elaborate. The following ideas will spark your imagination until you can create a beautiful setting for your event.

DON'T RAIN ON MY PARADE!

What's the first thing you think of when you think of rain showers? An umbrella, of course. Find a pretty one and use it for your decorations. Open it wide on a gift table and arrange the gifts under it. Set a pretty baby doll on top of the gifts. Find napkins featuring a cute baby under an umbrella. Perhaps you would also like to carry out this theme in your refreshments (look for ideas in chapter 7).

PRETTY BABY

Use a baby doll as a centerpiece for this shower decorating idea. Before the party ask invited guests to autograph a white diaper with permanent marking pens (use several colors). Add the date of the shower to the diaper and dress the doll in it. After the shower, give the doll to the honoree as a souvenir of her shower.

Center games and refreshments on the "pretty baby" idea, using babies everywhere.

SHOWER, ANYONE?

Have you had a shower lately—the wet kind? Use a shower nozzle as a decorating feature for this shower. Use a metal one or one of the colorful plastic spray nozzles that attach to tub outlets. Hang the nozzle high over the gift table. Attach narrow ribbons or string dipped in silver glitter to stream downward (like shower cascades of water) onto and around the table. Secure prizes for the games to the end of some of the streamers. Gifts will be nestled amid the "spray."

If a special hostess gift is given, a bathinette or items for the baby's bath would be appropriate.

LOOK WHAT THE STORK BROUGHT

Some department stores will loan the storks they use in their baby departments. Borrow one or more if you can. If you can borrow a tall one, stand him by or on the gift table. A smaller one could grace the serving table. From the bill of the stork, hang one of the following, depending on the size of the stork and what you have handy: a small basket; an inverted umbrella; a receiving blanket; or a diaper. Into whichever container you choose, put prizes, a small doll, or flowers. If you put a doll in the container, put a nurse's cap on your stork.

You may choose to attach an open umbrella over the stork's head and suspend a small gift from his bill.

Use information about how the stork entered the baby scene if you choose the stork motif. (See the stork section of the "Did You Know" theme in chapter 3.)

We Wish You Well

Create a "wishing well" for this decorating idea. Cover a large box with brick-patterned tissue or contact paper. Make a chain of large diaper pins. Fasten the chain to a diaper pail that sits down in the "brick" well. Guests will drop their small, lightweight gifts into the pail, to be drawn up by the chain at the gifting time. Larger, heavier gifts could be placed behind the well to be brought out when desired.

Carry out the "We wish you well" theme by giving each lady a large round paper "penny" on which she is to write her wish for the mother and baby. Those "pennies" can be thrown into the wishing well, too.

Flower Shower

This would be a good springtime decorating idea. Ask the decorating committee to "beg and borrow" flowers of all kinds from church ladies and neighbors. Borrow also vases other mothers were given when their babies were born. Fill the cute little vases shaped like bootees, cradles, blocks, and so forth, with fresh flowers and put them all around the fellowship hall or wherever you hold your shower. Add baby's breath to the arrangements. (See "Showers of Flowers" theme in chapter 2.)

Crepe Suzette

Festoon your fellowship hall with pink and blue crepe paper streamers. If yours is a rectangular room, center a gift table at one end and a serving table at the opposite end. Above each table drape arches of streamers twisted from the ceiling down to the edges of the tables. Attach small, lightweight prizes for game winners to the ends of the streamers at the gift table. If you wish, you can drape the entire hall with streamers, beginning at the ceiling center and draping to the walls with streamers about two feet apart.

PAMPER THE BABY

In these days when many modern mothers are looking for the convenience of disposable diapers, why not shower her with various brands of disposables? This will aid her budget and help her decide which kind she likes best. Coordinate with guests so all don't bring the same brand or size.

Since most brands feature a cuddly baby picture on their boxes, decorate your room with the biggest, cutest baby pictures you can find in magazines or borrow from local mothers.

Decorate a large box to look like a disposable diaper container, label it "Pamper Me!" and have guests place their gifts in it when they arrive. Refill it after gifts are opened for the mother-to-be's convenience in getting the gifts home.

On the wall behind the serving table arrange large pink and blue letters that read "Pamper the Pretty Baby." Nuts and mints served in diaper party favors are a must (see "Food and Favors" for directions).

Gifts for game winners (to be given to the honoree) could be powder, oil, and wet wipes—all to aid in pampering the baby's bottom.

SEASONAL SURPRISE SHOWERS

Have you a friend expecting a baby near Christmas time? Surprise her by inviting her to a Christmas party with a "white elephant" gift exchange. Tell all others (but not the honoree) to bring an additional gift appropriate to welcome a wee one.

Decorate in your traditional way or feature a lighted nativity scene on a table or mantle with glittered letters over it reminding guests, "God Loved Us and Sent His Son."

Invite guests to put their exchange gifts in a large paper bag, which has been put into a large red stocking. Baby gifts will be dropped behind the paper bag and down into the toe of the stocking. (Any gifts too large to fit into the stocking can be hidden in the hall closet as you take the guests' coats.)

At gift exchange time, each lady may select a gift from the sacked items in the stocking. When all have drawn a gift and it is obvious that the stocking is still not empty, ask guests what should be done with the remaining items. They, of course, will suggest they be given to the mother-to-be for whom you have arranged this surprise.

Refreshments could be seasonal or feature a birthday cake for Jesus. If you choose the latter, suggest to the future mother that she could begin on baby's first Christmas to tell the true meaning of Christmas by having a birthday celebration, complete with cake, each year, so her child can learn of the Savior very early in life.

As your devotional thought, read Luke 2:1-20 by candlelight. Try to feel anew the wonder Mary and Joseph felt at this holy birth. Relate this to the awe soon to be felt by your honoree as God blesses her in bringing forth a new life.

By exercising a little creativity, you can relate this seasonal surprise idea to most seasons and holidays. Consider the following and improvise:

Happy New Year—Bring in the new year (and new babe).

Easter—Welcome the new life.

Mother's Day Brunch—Welcome to the Royal Order of Motherhood.

Fourth of July—"We're getting a 'bang' out of your birth!" Serve popcorn and put sparklers on the cake. (Caution: protect your tablecloth from spark burns.)

Thanksgiving—"Thank You, God, for the baby."

Et cetera, et cetera!

THE LIGHT OF OUR LIFE

Have a candlelight shower. As a centerpiece, use one of those lovely large candles designed to be lighted at each birthday. These candles come in pink or blue and can be burned three to four hours each birthday until the twenty-first year. An eight-inch inexpensive candle is also available, colorful, pictoral with symbols fitting in blue for a boy or pink for a girl, covering sixteen years of birthdays.

Of course, you will give the candle to the honoree. Perhaps several guests would want to carry out the theme by giving "light" gifts—a lamp for the nursery, a glow-in-the-dark plaque, or a praying-child night light.

"Thy word is a lamp to my feet, and a light to my path" (Psalm 119:105) would be a fitting devotional thought to encourage the young mother to rear her child in the light of God's Word.

Baby Finds His Spot in the Sun

Does one in your circle of friends have a patio table protected from the sun by a bright outdoor umbrella? This would make an ideal setting for a small group spring or summer shower.

To "baby-fy" the scene, wrap the center post of the umbrella with alternating strips of pink and blue crepe paper. Hang alternately from the ribs of the umbrella several rattles and baby pictures (clipped from old cards and backed with pink and blue construction paper).

Decorate a child's wagon with crepe paper. Put gifts in. Have a child bring in the wagon carrying a decorated umbrella. Place the umbrella on the load of gifts when "parked" in front of the honoree.

Play a few sit-down games, serve simple, light refreshments, and enjoy "gifting" baby in the sun.

Easy Decorations

Pin large crepe paper bows on curtains. Pastel colored balloons hung on lamps and from the ceiling create a party atmosphere.

Make a canopy of crepe paper streamers for the honoree to sit under. Fasten to ceiling with scotch tape; twirl two colors together and fasten to the floor with a bit of tape. If the room is carpeted, use a pin, tack, or weights. Or have the streamers come down from a light fixture to make a canopy for the mother-to-be.

Decorate the table with crepe paper streamers twirled and

coming down from the chandelier to the center of the table or to the corners. Or put a twirled paper streamer down the middle of the table.

Put an arrangement of flowers or a plant in a child's "potty" for a cute table centerpiece. Spray a graceful dry branch pink or blue, put in a vase and hang small baby toys from its twigs. Baby dolls and stuffed animals make darling decorations also.

7

Food and Favors

Food and fun go together. Your refreshments can be as simple or as elaborate as your kitchen committee desires. "Fix ahead" recipes follow to free the cooks to enjoy the festivities, too.

SIMPLE DESSERT-TYPE RECIPES

Orange Muffins

1 cup sugar
1 cup margarine
4 beaten eggs
1 cup white corn syrup
½ cup milk

4 cups flour sifted with 2 t.
  soda, 2 t. salt
½ cup chopped nuts
½ cup chopped dates or raisins
1 6-oz. can frozen orange juice

Mix all ingredients in order. Fill muffin tins ⅔ full. Bake at 350 degrees for 25 or 30 minutes. This batter can be stored in the refrigerator for up to a month.

Rhubarb Nut Bread

1½ cups brown sugar
⅔ cup oil
1 egg
2¾ cups flour
1 t. soda
1 t. salt

1 cup buttermilk
1 t. vanilla
1½ cups diced rhubarb
½ cup walnuts
Topping: ⅓ cup sugar, 1 T.
  butter, cinnamon

73

Mix brown sugar, oil, and egg. Add flour, soda, salt. Stir in buttermilk and vanilla. Fold in rhubarb and nuts. Pour into two greased loaf pans. Sprinkle topping over dough. Bake 350 degrees for 45 minutes.

Julie's Banana Split Dessert

graham cracker crust
2 cups powdered sugar
2 eggs
1 cup margarine

3 to 5 sliced bananas
2 cups fresh strawberries
8-oz. crushed pineapple, drained
2 cups whipped cream, or 9-oz. container of Cool Whip
Chocolate syrup, chopped nuts

Press a graham cracker crust into a 9 by 13-inch pan. Beat sugar, eggs, and margarine for 15 minutes. Spread onto crust. Layer on top of mixture bananas, strawberries, and pineapple. Spread whipped cream or Cool Whip on top. Drizzle with chocolate syrup and a few nuts. Refrigerate.

Marion's Heavenly Pie

18 graham crackers
1 cup butter or margarine
3 cups powdered sugar
4 eggs

2 8-oz. cans crushed pineapple, drained
2 cups heavy cream, whipped

Crush graham crackers, spread in 9 by 13-inch pan, reserving some crumbs for top. Mix butter, powdered sugar, and eggs; spoon mixture onto cracker crumb crust. Fold pineapple into cream; spread over first layer. Sprinkle with remaining crumbs.

Shirley's Shortcake

2 cups flour
3 t. baking powder
½ t. salt
4 T. shortening (rounded)

1 T. sugar (if desired)
⅔ cup milk
berries
whipped topping, if desired

74

Combine dry ingredients; cut in shortening with two knives or pastry blender. Blend in ⅔ cup milk. Knead briefly. Roll out one inch high. Cut and bake for 12 minutes at 425 degrees. Top with sugared strawberries or raspberries and whipped topping.

Fruit Cocktail Dessert

1 cup sifted flour
1 cup sugar
1 t. soda
½ t. salt

1 no. 2 can fruit cocktail
1 egg, beaten
½ cup chopped nuts
½ cup brown sugar

Sift together first four ingredients. Combine fruit cocktail with beaten egg and add to dry ingredients. Mix well. Sprinkle nut and brown sugar mixture on top. Bake in 8-inch square pan at 350 degrees for 45 minutes.

Frozen Strawberry Dessert

Crust:
½ cup butter (margarine)
1 cup flour
1 t. vanilla

¼ cup brown sugar
½ cup nuts

Filling:
10-oz. package frozen
    strawberries
2 egg whites
2 T. lemon juice

1 cup sugar
1 c. whipping cream
1 t. vanilla

Mix crust ingredients. Pat into a 9 by 13-inch pan. Bake 20 to 30 minutes at 350 degrees. While baking, stir twice. Save ¼ of crumbs for top.

Beat filling ingredients in large bowl for about 15 minutes or until thick.

Fold in 1 cup of whipping cream that has been whipped with 1 t. vanilla. Put filling over crumb crust. Top with remaining crumbs. Freeze.

Peanut Butter Squares

1 cup sugar
1 cup light corn syrup
1 cup crunchy peanut butter
5 cups rice cereal
1 cup salted peanuts
1 6-oz. pkg. chocolate chips

Bring sugar and corn syrup to a boil, stirring to dissolve sugar. Remove from heat and stir in peanut butter. Pour over cereal and nuts in buttered bowl. Mix well. Pat into buttered 9 by 13-inch pan. Melt chips and spread over the top. Cool and cut into squares.

Peach Bavarian

1 3-oz. package peach gelatin
¼ cup sugar
1 cup boiling water
¾ cup cold water or fruit juice
1 envelope whipped topping mix or 1 cup whipped cream

Dissolve gelatin and sugar in boiling water. Add cold water. Chill until slightly thickened. Prepare the topping mix as directed on package or whip the cream; stir 1½ cups into gelatin until blended. Pour into a 1-quart mold or bowl, or 6 to 8 serving dishes. Chill until firm. To serve, unmold and garnish with remaining whipped topping. Serves 6 to 8.

Strawberry Cake

(A pretty, "pink-for-a-girl," easy-to-prepare dessert for your shower.)

Mix together:

1 white cake mix
1 pkg. strawberry jello (3 oz.)
1 cup oil
½ cup water
¾ cup strawberries
4 eggs

Bake in a floured, greased 9 by 13-inch pan at 375 degrees for about 30 minutes. Frost when cool with the following: a mixture of ¼ cup strawberries, 1 stick margarine (melted), 1 pound powdered sugar. Note: A 10-oz. package of frozen strawberries works fine. Thaw them, reserve ¼ cup for the frosting, and dump the rest into the cake batter. Serves 24.

76

Magic Cookie Bars

Melt in 9 by 13-inch pan: ½ cup margarine.

Add: 1 cup graham cracker crumbs, 1 cup coconut, 1 cup chocolate chips, 1 cup butterscotch chips, ½ cup nuts (optional).

Pour over this in pan: 1 can sweetened condensed milk (Eagle Brand). Bake 25 minutes at 350 degrees. Cool and cut into bars.

ELABORATE EDIBLES

Many items are available for the creative cook who likes to decorate elaborately. Check with a hobby store or consult a cake decorating catalog. You can buy plastic, edible, and reusable items. Look for storks, rattles, baby buntings, and bootees on picks and chenille stems. Tiny plastic and sugar buggies, cribs, babies, rattles, storks, and bootees can be found. Complete tops for instant decoration and reusable decorating kits can be bought for a reasonable price. With those, a simple sheet cake can become a beautiful edible centerpiece for a shower. Shaped cake pans are also for sale. The lamb-shaped pan would make an adorable treat to welcome a precious "little lamb."

Cut-up cakes look difficult but really are not. Try these hints to make funtime cut-up cakes. Cool cakes on cloth-covered racks, top side up. If you freeze them they can be cut in shapes and frosted easier. Easy-to-follow instructions are given in *Betty Crocker's Cake and Frosting Mix Cookbook* (New York: Golden Press, 1966) for making twin cradle cakes, baby bootees, candy umbrellas, and an umbrella cake. These and many other ideas make the purchase of this simplified book a good investment.

Decorator's Frosting

Beat together:

4 oz. cream cheese	¾ lb. Crisco
1 cube butter	1 t. vanilla
¼ t. salt	powdered sugar

Sift powdered sugar into the above creamy mixture until frosting is thick and manageable. Add the sugar gradually. Color with food coloring. (This frosting tastes good! If you wish to frost the entire cake with it, add 2 to 4 tablespoons of hot water to make it spreadable.)

Teddy Bear Cake

Prepare your favorite "scratch" or mix cake. Bake in an 8-inch round pan and a 9-inch square pan. Freeze cooled cakes to facilitate cutting in shapes. Cut the square cake like this:

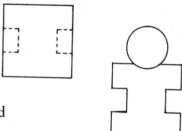

Put the pieces and round cake together on a tray.

Prepare 7-minute frosting for white face, tummy, and paws. Melt 1 package of sweet chocolate. Put 2 tablespoons of it into the white frosting. Frost the rest of the cake. Coat coconut with remaining chocolate. Chill. Sprinkle the chocolate coconut on the dark parts of the bear and plain white coconut on the white parts. Finish the bear with cookies and candy as illustrated.

Ears—chocolate cookies

Eyes—white mints, green gumdrop pupils

Nose, navel—black gumdrops

Red sucker

Mouth, pawnails— licorice rope

Tongue—red gumdrop

Baby Jacket Cake

Bake a one-layer 9 by 13 inch cake and cut it as illustrated. Frost and finish as desired in pastels, lace, and roses.

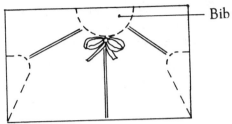

To make a small bib, save the small half-circle on the long side which was cut for the neck hole. Edge and decorate as desired with frosting. Attach a ribbon if desired. A message of welcome could be typed on a card or piped onto the cake board. *

Crowd-Sized Bootee Cake

Bake the foot part of the bootee in a 5-pound ham can and the leg part in a 3-pound shortening can. When cake is cool, stack the leg part on the foot part as sketched and decorate as you wish with frosting, roses, and ribbon. To serve: cut the "toe" lengthwise to the base of the "leg," then slice across. Cut the leg in half horizontally. Set the halves beside each other and slice as you would any other round cake. (See illustration.)

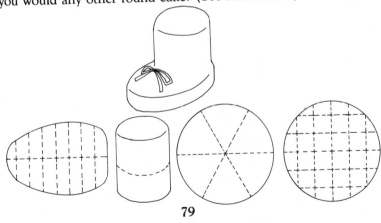

79

*Courtesy MAIL BOX NEWS, Maid of Scandinavia, Minneapolis, Minn. 55416

Bib and Tucker

Make a large bib cake for your shower. Bake your batter in a 10-inch round pan. Cut out a 4-inch circle for the neck. Place cake on a round serving plate with a border of ruffling under the cake. Decorate as desired with frosting and ribbon. If you know the names chosen by your honoree you may want to frost them on the bib.

Baby Buggy Beauty

This difficult-looking cake is so simple to make. Bake half your cake batter in a round pan and the other half in a small cup cake pan. When cool, imagine the cake to be a pie divided in sixths and cut out a one-sixth wedge as sketched. Use two cup cakes for wheels. Slice off their tops, if need be, to make them the same thickness as the buggy.

Frost as desired, giving the buggy a wickerwork appearance and spoking the wheels. Attach a long, curved chenille stem for the buggy handle.

Fruity Umbrellas

To embellish a plain cake, add an umbrella or two made of lemon, orange, or lime slices. Slice the fruit you select (according to color and size of umbrella) in thin slices with the rind still attached. Cut each slice in half. Make the handle of skin removed from the other half of the slice. These umbrellas can march around the sides of your cake or sit atop it. Pretty and edible.

EDIBLE FAVORS

Tiny Baby Buggies

For each buggy use one candy orange slice, four Lifesavers and part of a pipe cleaner. Arrange as shown, holding "wheels" on with toothpicks.

Candy Bootees or Storks

Buy molds for making candy mints. Most hobby stores have them. Use this easy recipe for delicious decorative candy bootees or storks.

3-oz. pkg. cream cheese   ¼ t. flavoring
2½ cups unsifted powdered sugar (measured before sifting)
Color as desired.

Cream the cheese at room temperature. Add flavor and desired color. Blend well. Add sifted sugar. Work well with hands. Roll into marble sized balls. Dip each ball into a small amount of granulated sugar. Press into sugared mold, sugar side down. Turn mold upside down to release mint on waxed paper. Refrigerate the mints until ready to serve.

Flavoring hints: Use white vanilla for making storks and mint or strawberry flavor for making green or pink bootees. This recipe makes about 8 dozen storks or 100 bootees.

THIRST QUENCHERS

Steaming tea or coffee fill the bill for most gatherings. If you want to serve a pretty, nutritious fruit punch, try one of these.

Orange Pepper
For every two servings, beat together 1 t. honey and 1 cup of orange juice. (Frozen orange juice can be substituted.) Serve with chipped ice in frosty glasses.

Hot Percolator Punch
2½ cups unsweetened pineapple juice   1½ t. whole cloves
2 cups cranberry juice   1½ t. whole allspice
½ cup water   3 sticks cinnamon,
⅓ cup dark brown sugar, packed   broken into pieces

Place liquids in percolator. Put sugar and spices in the basket of the percolator. Percolate 10 to 12 minutes. Serve while hot. Serves 12.

Fluffy Pink Punch
2 pints soft raspberry sherbert
1 quart ginger ale (or citrus soda)
¼ cup lemon juice

Put the sherbert in punch bowl. Pour liquids over sherbert. Break up the sherbert gently. Makes 16 one-half cup servings.

Rosy Fruit Punch

1 cup strong undiluted tea (about 4 tea bags)
1½ cups sugar (or to taste)
2 6-oz. cans frozen pineapple juice
1 6-oz. can frozen orange juice
2 6-oz. cans frozen lemon juice
2 pkg. strawberry powdered drink mix
1 quart ginger ale
1 10-oz. pkg. frozen strawberries
Red food color

Mix together, adding water according to directions on cans or packages. Add food color as desired to get just the shade of pink you prefer. Float the strawberries on top. Serves 35.

Lo-Cal Rosy Fruit Punch

To lower the calorie count in the above punch recipe, substitute: low calorie sweetener in place of sugar, low calorie pop in place of ginger ale, low calorie Hawaiian punch in place of powdered drink mix.

Delicious, and will help the mother-to-be to keep her weight in control.

8

Financial Finaglings

Is your group having a baby boom and a budget bust simultaneously? These ideas may help you entertain more economically.

PRICELESS INVITATIONS

Ask ladies to help you collect old baby cards, shower invitations, baby shower gift-wrap paper, or magazine pictures of babies. Recycle those castoffs into invitations to the shower you have planned. Cut away past evidences of use and write the invitation on what is left. Or glue pictures onto plain index cards or pastel memo sheets, and write in the facts.

Make your invitations with napkins. Fold a small pastel-colored napkin into a diaper triangle and fasten with a tiny gold safety pin. Slip a card inside that reads, "For Sue's Project in the Three-cornered Pants" and gives the time and place of the shower.

Try a cloth invitation. Cut small triangles with pinking shears from an old sheet. Fold these into tiny diapers secured with small gilt pins. Tuck a fact sheet inside each diaper and distribute to guests-to-be. Be sure to save one for the honoree, who doubtless will want to keep one for her baby book.

Invite ladies to your shower with marshmallow booties glued to a card that reads:

We'll soon hear the patter of little feet.
Friends want to help the expenses to meet.
    Time: Place: Honoree:

Make these simple booties by using miniature pastel marshmallows. If you'd like bigger booties, use the large marshmallows and frost them in pastel shades of icing.

Cut out baby carriage shapes, some pink and some blue. On the front side draw a large question mark where the baby's head should be in the carriage. On the back print shower details.

Other economy invitations can be made from wallpaper samples. Ask at stores for old wallpaper sample books. Most of them have patterns appropriate to nurseries. Those pages can be cut up and the invitation printed on the back of the paper. Or pictures from the wallpaper can decorate index card invitations.

HALL OF FAME GREETINGS

Original greetings to treasure are always appreciated when women who are skilled at art and crafts draw, paint, sketch, stencil, needlepoint, or découpage their cards to welcome the new baby.

Try this economy original greeting card to accompany your shower gift. Get a wallpaper sample book. Find a nursery pattern. Tear the wallpaper into shapes to fold up like a card. Write this little message on the inside:

Since saving money is so hard,
    and cost of living high,
A pretty, fancy baby card
    we can't afford to buy.
Not to send you baby greetings
    would never do at all.
So to wish you happy parenting
    we tore the paper off the wall!

Ladies talented in writing prose or poetry can produce treasured "hall of fame" greetings to make the recipient feel her baby is indeed special.

Original Birth Announcements

Originality is appreciated when it comes from the honoree too. Perhaps you would like to suggest she consider patterning her child's birth announcement after one of these "originals." Better still, these may get her creativity stirring so that she will dream up an even cuter idea.

BABYGRAM

This announcement is patterned after a telegram. Type the message in capital letters on the yellow "babygram" form, as shown.

$_____ a day   Dr. _____

_____ ¢ a quart   R.N. _____

$_____ office call

By Mail Train, Truck, Bus, Foot

DATE

TIME

HOSPITAL, TOWN

MR. AND MRS. RELATIVE OR FRIEND

HAVE DAUGHTER. WILL BRAG. NAMED _____.

WEIGHS _____. _____ INCHES LONG.

LOVE,

PARENTS' NAME

AN ORIGINAL MOTOR

The E. D. Northington Company of St. Joseph, Missouri

Incorporated _____ (marriage date)

F.O.B. St. Luke's Hospital

Kansas City, Missouri

Ami Linn Northington

Model No. 1 Released December 17, 1979

Chassis Weight 5 lbs. 14 oz.

Chief Engineer	Mr. E. D. Northington
Production Manager	Mrs. Vicki Northington
Technical Advisor	Doctor Gary Lockwood

Special Features

two lung power   changeable seat covers

runs on 1 quart milk a day

knee action   free squealing

Must be heard to be appreciated. On display at: _____Parents

_____Address

Management guarantees no other 1979 model.

(A similar announcement adds these special features to the above: scream line body, double bawl bearing, and water cooled exhaust.)

A COLOR ORIGINAL

From Louisiana comes this idea: the outline of the state folded and cut from manila art paper and colored by the new baby's big sister, aged seven. Outline your state and use your state bird.

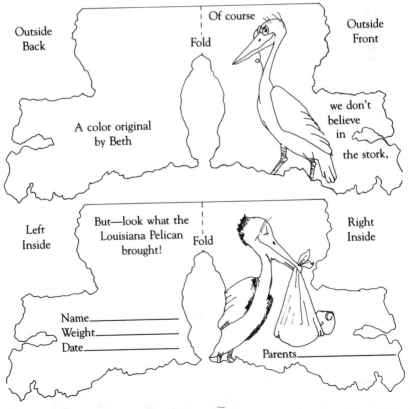

Outside Back   Of course   Fold   Outside Front

we don't believe in the stork,

A color original by Beth

Left Inside   But—look what the Louisiana Pelican brought!   Fold   Right Inside

Name_____

Weight_____

Date_____

Parents_____

REPORT CARD

A teacher sent out her baby's first report card, neatly manuscript-printed on yellow construction paper and labeled on back as an ABC card, "Another Beautiful Child!" A cute baby cut from gift wrapping graced the outer cover. The inside informed as follows:

Birth Report Card	(Fold)	Grading Symbols
Name_____		E—Excellent
		N—Needs Improvement
Address_____		S—Satisfactory
Parents_____		*Health*
		Weight ___ lbs. ___ oz.
Sister_____		Height ___ in.
		Keeps neat and clean S
We feel our new pupil is making excellent progress considering the number of class hours that are spent asleep.		*Activities*
		Eating S
		Smiling S
		Crying E
		Staying Dry N
		Sleeping at Night N
		Attendance
		Date entered_____
		(birth date)
		Days tardy_____
		(past due date)

OUR PRIVATE MIRACLE

Can the new mother or dad draw well? Perhaps as they gaze with love upon the miracle of their love, the artist would like to sketch their baby and accompany their reproduction with the caption: "This is now bone of my bones, and flesh of my flesh" (Genesis 2:23). A friend with an offset press could economically print this treasured card for mailing to friends.

A later sketch of the baby could become part of an original "thank you" card.

A NEW ADDITION

ANNOUNCING A NEW ADDITION TO
THE CARLSON HOME
June 26, 1980   10:11 A.M.

Designer and Builder:	God Almighty
Title Holders:	Myron and Carolee Carlson
Interest Holder:	Libby Carlson
Title:	Priscilla Jean Carlson (Ellie)
Dimensions:	8 lbs. 10½ oz., 21½ inches
Description:	Light brown hair, dark eyes
Taxes:	Reduced due to added exemption
Discipline:	2 × 4's

Care and Maintenance Requirements:

Frequent communication with Builder

Sense of humor

Unselfishness

Patience

Blanket insulation

SOUVENIRS

Every new mother would love to have a souvenir of her shower. Baby books are expensive, and she may already have one. Make her a treasured keepsake with odds and ends of cloth, lace, ribbon, paper, pictures, and glue.

Use a scrap of cloth pretty for a baby. Tiny checks or animal print are perfect. The size of the cloth will determine the size of your book. Eight by ten or nine by twelve inches are nice sizes. Cut a piece of poster board, corrugated board, or cracker box the chosen size. Cover it on the top side with cotton batting or old nylons for softness. Stretch the cloth over the cardboard covering top and bottom sides. Secure the cloth with glue or sewing. Fold the cover, book fashion. Hand stitch an edging of lace around the book. Glue a pretty baby picture edged in lace on the top cover. Fold five or six pages of typing paper inside the book for pages. Fasten those in with ribbon that you can tie on the outside of the book. Label pages for guest list, gifts, program, games, food, favors, and any other feature you think the honoree might want to include. A page or two with pockets would be nice to hold cards received. (Make by taping a third of a sheet on the bottom and side edges of the page.) Pictures from old cards beautify the pages.

Is your honoree one who likes to keep every little thing? If so, she will want to keep the paper and bows from her shower. Bows can be part of the shower fun. As they are removed from gifts, a friend can arrange them on a paper plate she is making into a bonnet for the honoree to wear at the party. Longer ribbons can be streamers with which to tie the hat on.

Bows are pretty tied on a coat hanger to hang in baby's closet. A clear plastic garment bag will keep free of dust.

Perhaps a friend would like to make a net bow-holder. Sew two squares of net together leaving an opening for the bows to be inserted. A net pillow is a nice bed or crib accent.

Paper is often kept to line the baby's chest of drawers. But you might want to use some of it to make a one-of-a-kind scrapbook the new mother will treasure forever. Before the shower, ask each lady to bring an article she has read on child care, a significant or humorous poem, or a note of personal advice for the new mother. Collect those when they arrive. After the gifts are opened, cut page-size pieces from the gift wrapping paper. Assemble them into pages of a notebook binder or your own prepared-ahead-of-time scrapbook folder.

Nut Cups and Favors

These take-home favors are such nice reminders of the special occasions showers are. Ladies who enjoy crafts are quick to volunteer to make these fun items.

CRADLE NUT CUP

Use the following outline, some construction paper, glue, and ribbon to make this cute cradle.

Cut two cradle boards.

A (cut)	Fold inward	D (cut)
B	Fold Fold	E
(cut)	Fold inward	(cut)
C		F

Glue ribbon on head cradle board.

Cut on dotted lines. Fold on fold lines. Fold and glue A and C over B and D and F over E to form bed. Glue cradle board on the ends. Fill with nuts and mints.

DANDY DIDIES

Cut pastel-colored flannel into triangles 4 by 4 by 6 inches with pinking shears. Fold these diaper style and fasten with a small gilt pin. Fill with candies and nuts. For firmer diapers, dip each into melted parafin and let harden before use.

Less permanent diaper nut cups can be made with small napkins. Select a pastel, baby shower, or floral napkin. Fold one corner over to make the triangle. Pin, and you are ready to fill your colorful table favor.

STORK FAVOR

A clever, inexpensive, decorative take-home favor can be made with a twist of the wrist. Take a large safety pin, a pink toothpick, and a snip of pink and blue ribbon. Create Mr. Stork by opening the pin, tying the ribbon in the curl of the tail end of the pin, bending the pin to form a neck, and pushing half a toothpick into the fastener on the head of the pin. Your finished product should look somewhat like a stork standing on one leg. He'll look quite perky perched on each individual piece of cake.

You may need to get your husband to help you bend the pins.

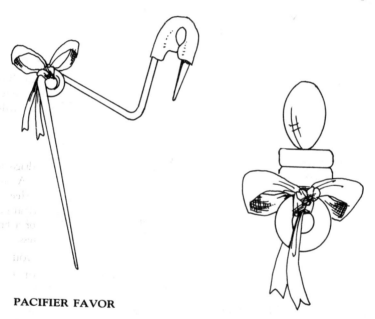

PACIFIER FAVOR

For each favor, cut a 9-inch length of narrow pink or blue ribbon. Slip the ribbon through the hole of a Lifesaver candy and tie it in a bow. Stick a long straight pin into the middle of the bow with the point sticking up. Lay 2 more Lifesavers over the pin. Push a pink or yellow jelly bean onto the pin. Each guest will want one of these "pacifiers."

Money-Saving Napkins

Fancy patterned napkins, decorated paper plates and doilies are often expensive throw-aways. Cut your expenses by using cheaper plain white or pastel-colored napkins. But be original with them.

Make your plain napkin something money can't buy by cutting it like a baby kimono as sketched.

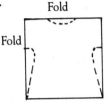

Eliminate the need for a doily and plate by serving your cake on a napkin folded like this:

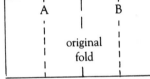

1. Open napkin to form long rectangle.

2. Fold A and B in half to meet original fold line.

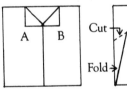

3. Fold upper tips of A and B down to form collar.

4. Cut a diagonal slant on A and B for sleeve. Fold triangle under for a finished dress.

Be sure to fold more napkins than the number of guests you expect. These are so cute some ladies will want an extra for a souvenir.

Wrap It Up

Save yourself the money gift-wrapping paper costs and let your wrapper also be a clue to what the gift is. Try wrapping a gift of diapers in one of the diapers. Instead of spending money on bows, decorate the package with a cute rattle or pacifier baby can use.

Receiving blankets also make pretty, usable wrappings.

Wrap a small gift with a page from the calendar. Circle the baby's birthdate on the calendar with a red Magic Marker.

ECONOMICAL GIFTING

Anything made by the giver is a special treasure to the receiver. Many women talented at knitting and crocheting keep their nimble fingers flying during most sitting moments and have on hand at all times economical gifts of bootees and sweater sets. Others stitch up blankets, kimonos, and sleepers.

A simple but useful item one can make with the sewing machine is a hooded baby towel.

HOODED BABY TOWEL

Materials Needed:

1 yard of soft terry cloth or 1 soft bath towel
4 yards wide binding tape of contrasting color
1 washcloth (same color as the towel)

Fold the washcloth in half. Pin the point of the washcloth in one corner of the towel (or terry cloth). Machine stitch the binding around the outside of the towel, attaching the washcloth to form a hood (see sketch).

Following are gift suggestions for the arts-and-crafts enthusiast. They are useful for decorating the nursery.

NURSERY WALL PLAQUES

Have you seen a cute napkin? Frame it for a one-of-a-kind gift. Or make a pair to decorate the nursery wall.

Materials Needed:

White foam shape — oval, circle, or square

Picture from napkin

Diamond Dust

White clear-drying glue

Ribbon

Lay the foam shape on newspaper. Separate the layers of your napkin, using only the top layer of paper. Cut the design you want from the napkin. Pour some glue into a dish. Thin it with a few drops of water. Brush a coat of glue on the side of the foam plaque shape. Lay the napkin design on the desired place on the foam, printed side up, and apply a second coat of glue. Wrinkles that may appear will not show on the completed plaque. Sprinkle a thin coat of Diamond Dust over the entire glued area and let it dry.

Encircle the dried plaque with ribbon, securing it with glue or pins. A matching bow may be made at the top of the plaque.

FOAM BABY-BOOK

This display item is made like the nursery plaque except the picture, poem, or birth announcement is mounted on a white foam book shape. The finished book can lie flat or lean on a stand.

NEWBORN SHADOW BOX

This treasure would have to be made by a friend after the baby is born. In a purchased or homemade shadow box, arrange in the compartments the birth announcement, the hospital bracelet, a picture of the newborn babe, tiny bootees (stuffed), a rattle, some baby's breath, and other keepsakes as compartments allow.

9
FRUITFUL FUTURES

The Lord told Adam and Eve to "be fruitful and multiply" (Genesis 1:28). Mankind continues to follow their example of bringing little ones into our world. We know not what the future holds, but we do know Who holds the future. Those of us who know the Creator and Sustainer of all life need to work together to help humans (who participate with God in creating the lives of the future) to mold those lives after His biddings. Having a shower with Christian love is a timely way of saying, "We want to help you give this little one a fruitful future with the Father."

Who can measure the effect of a lovingly-given baby shower? It is an opportunity for a caring church group or individuals to remind a young mother of the Lord at the time when she is most softened to Him through fear of the future for her unborn child.

The authors of this "how to" book pray the Lord will bless our efforts and yours as we seek together to make the events surrounding each new arrival a special welcome into God's world. May we remember to help each new family lead their little ones to faith in Christ.

We pray God's Showers of Blessings upon you!

Moody Press, a ministry of the Moody Bible Institute, is designed for education, evangelization, and edification. If we may assist you in knowing more about Christ and the Christian life, please write us without obligation: Moody Press, c/o MLM, Chicago, Illinois 60610.